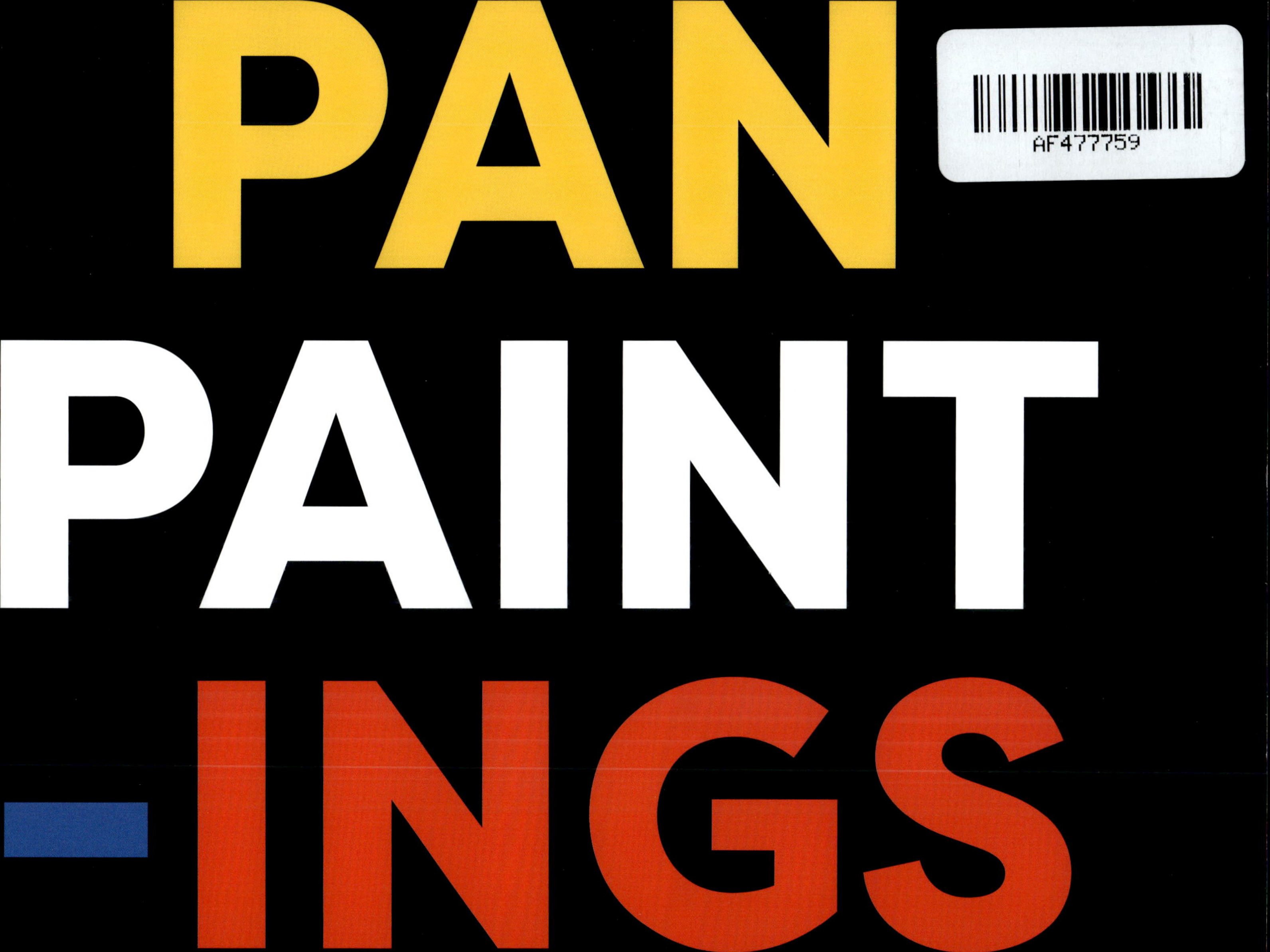

PAN
PAINT
-INGS
AF477759

Untitled (pan painting), 2014

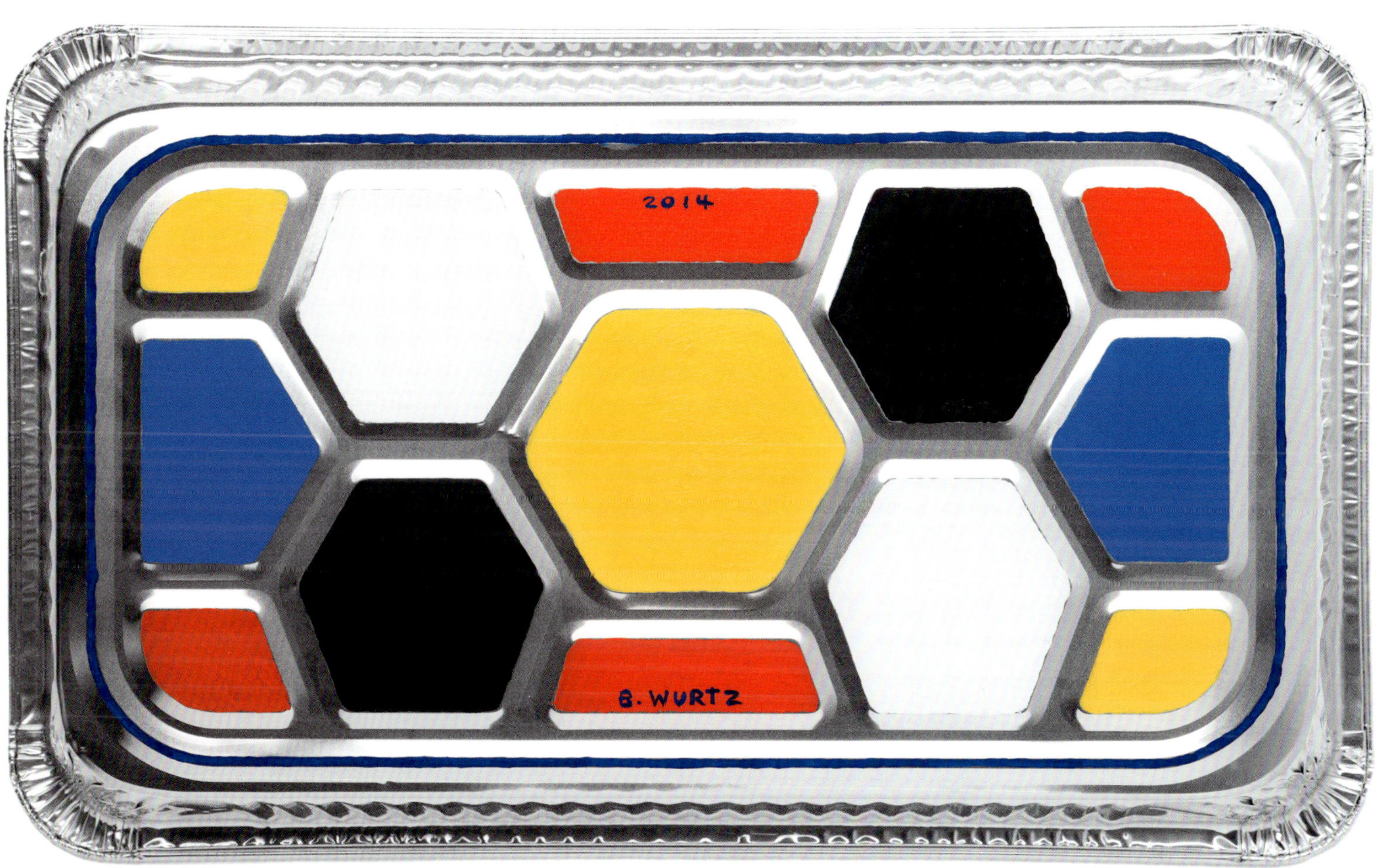

2014
B. WURTZ

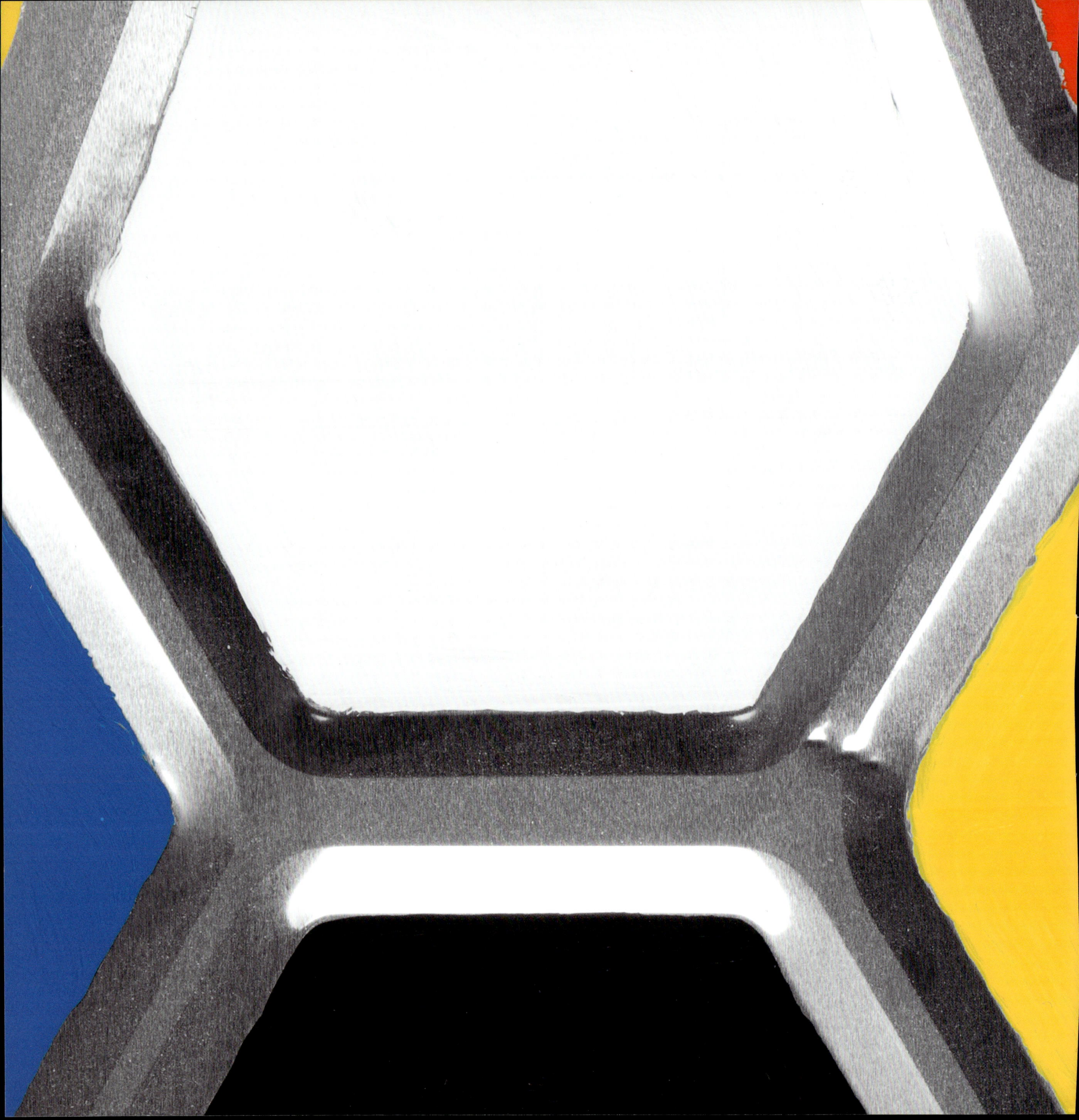

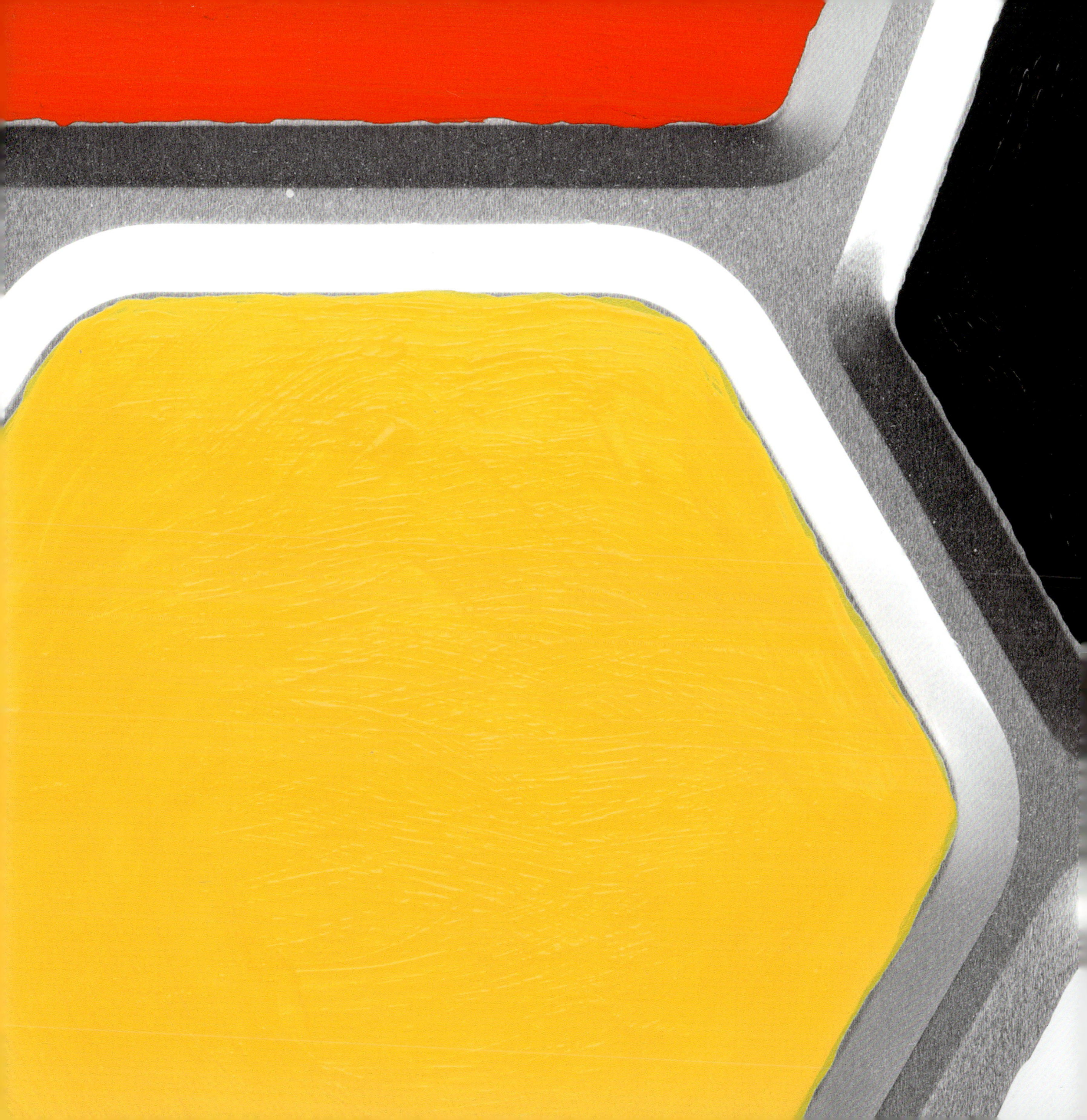

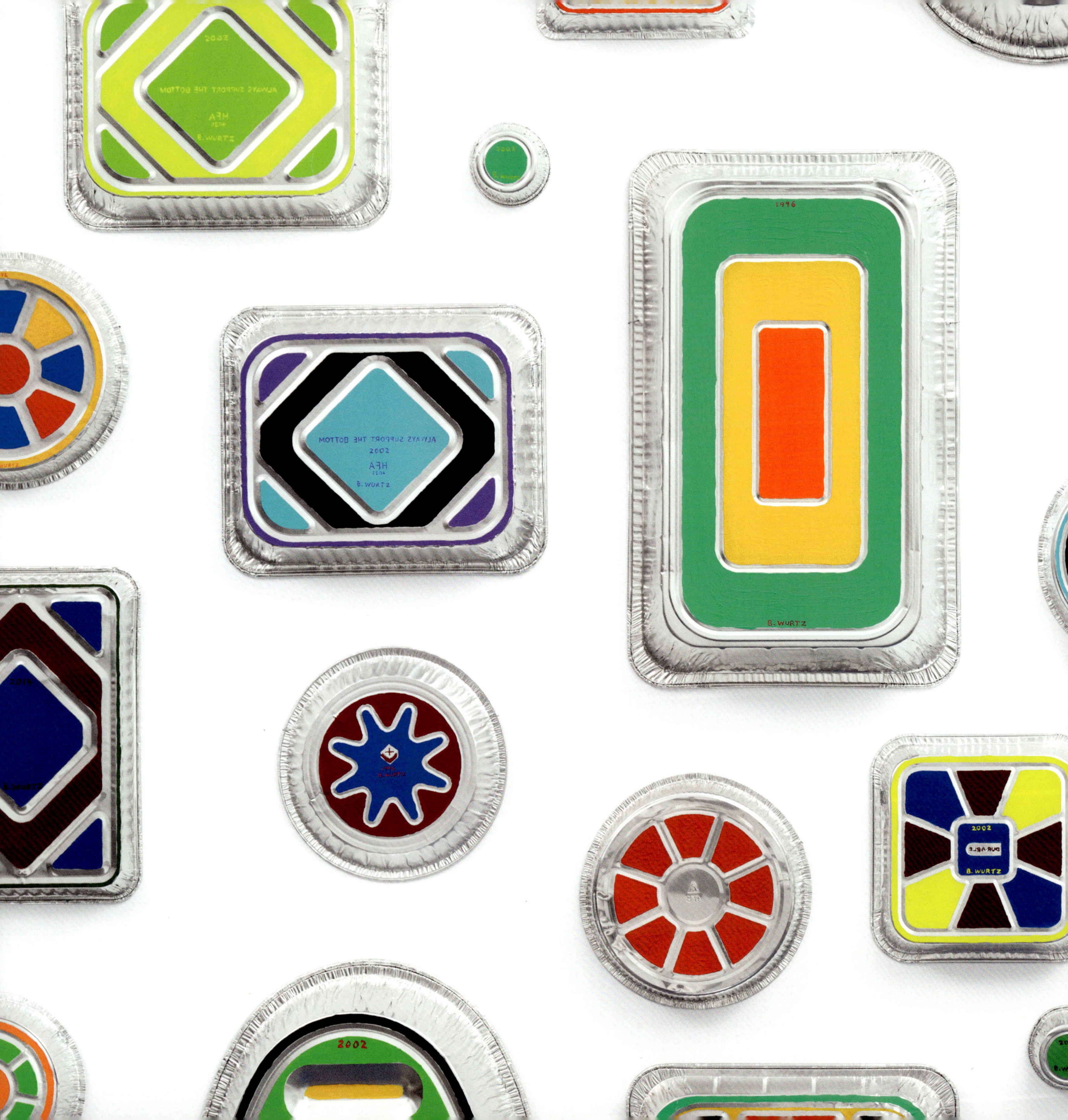

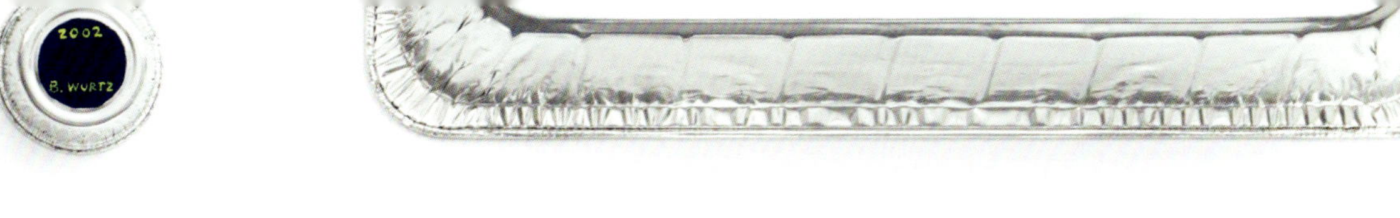
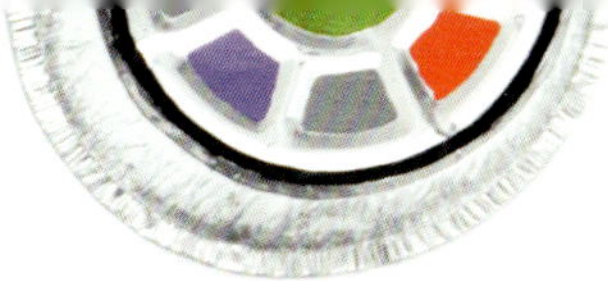
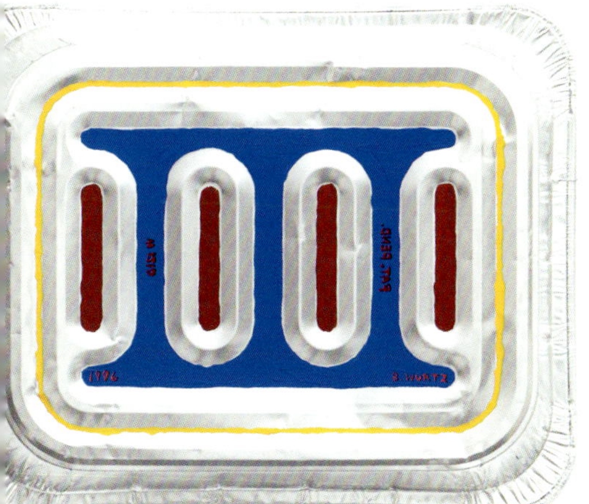
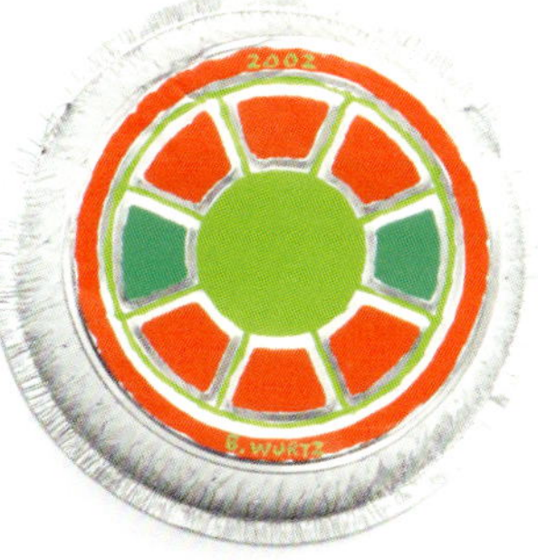
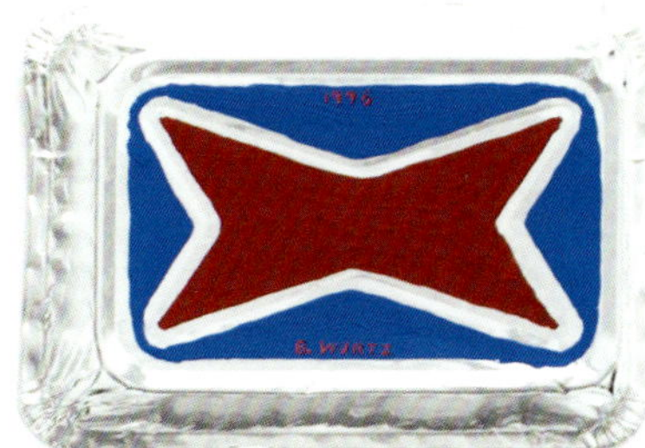
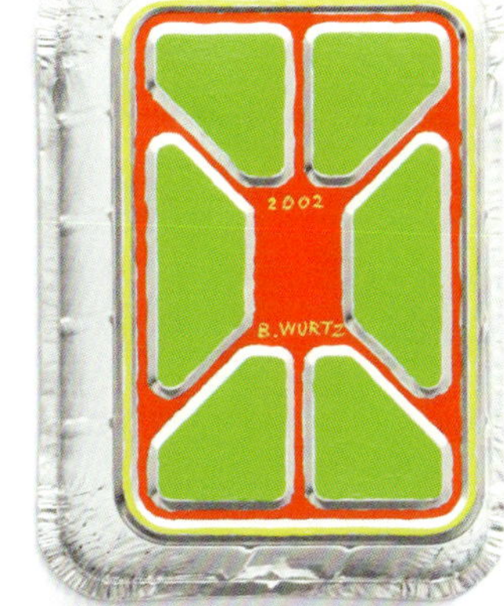
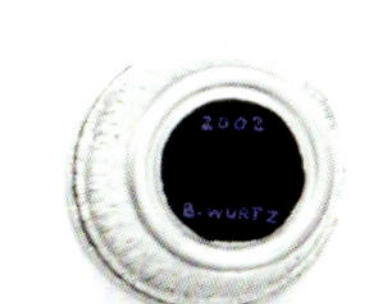
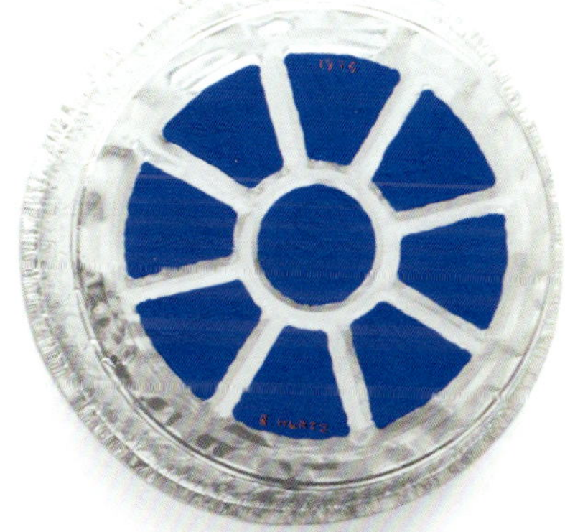
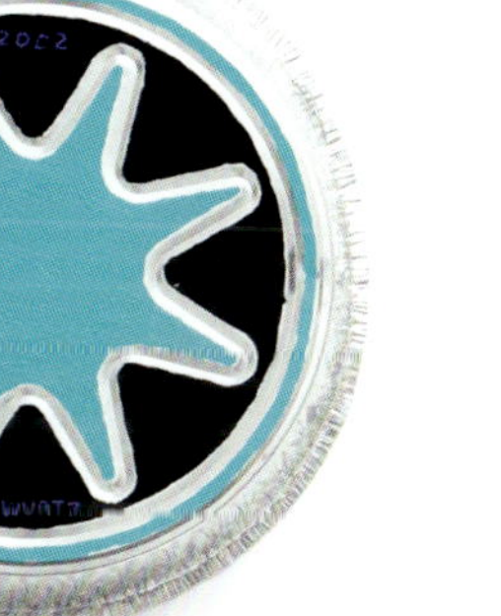
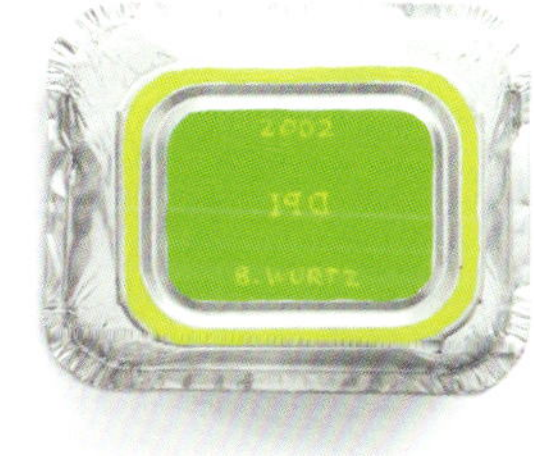
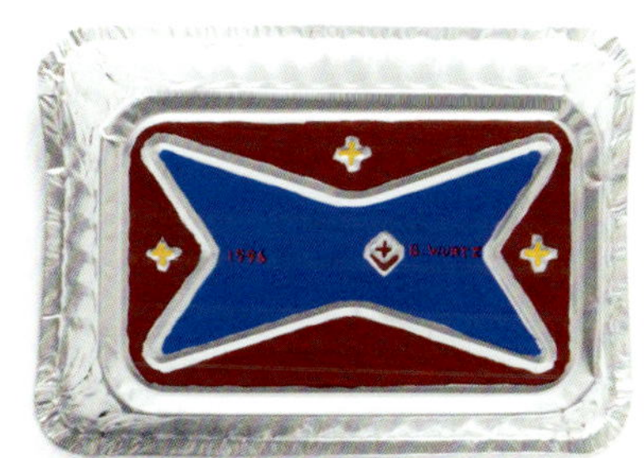
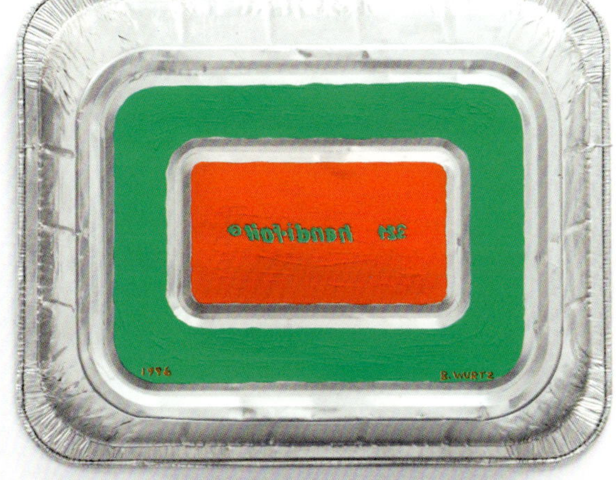
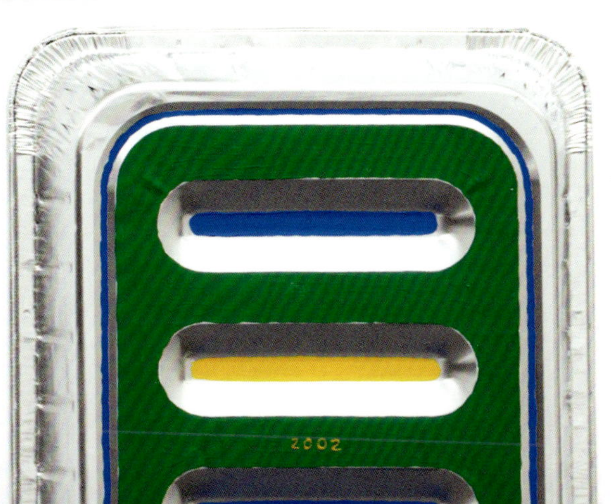
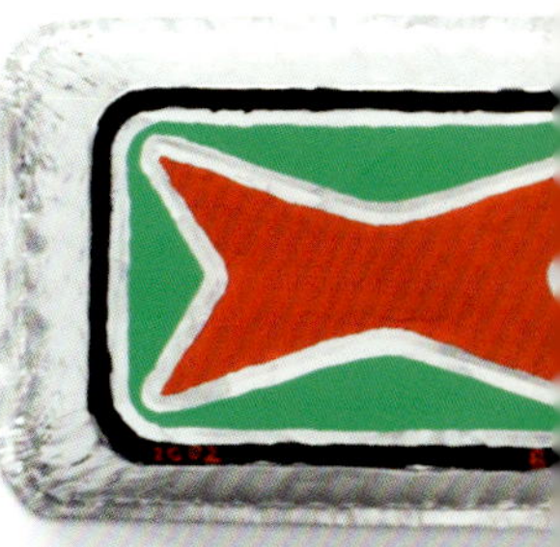

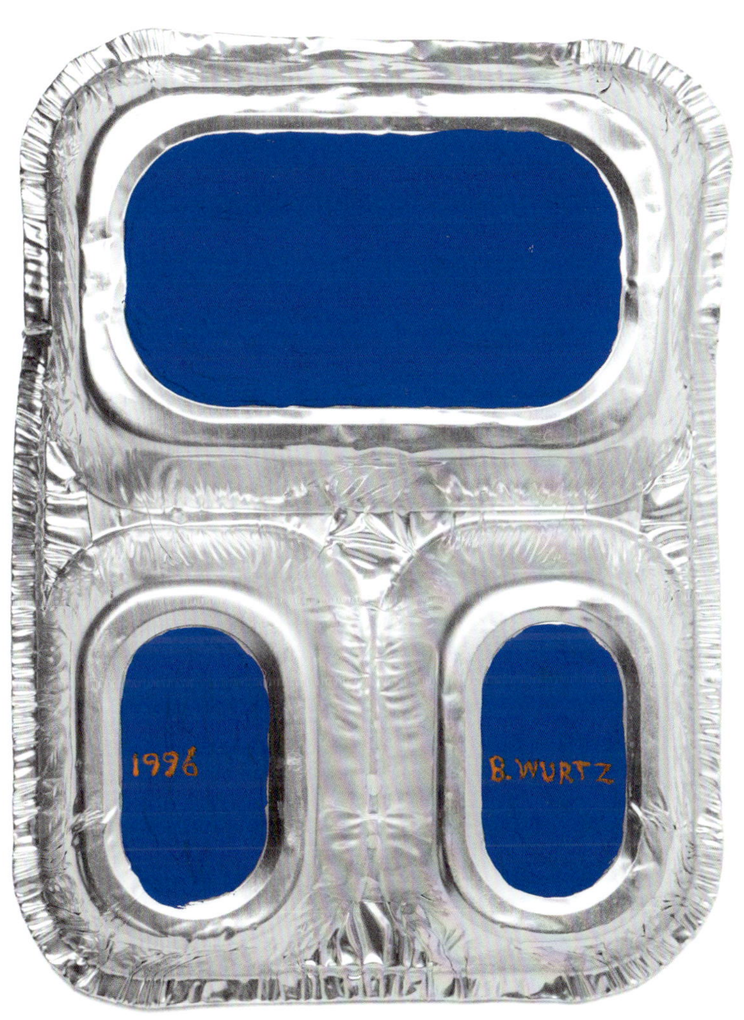

1996
B. WURTZ

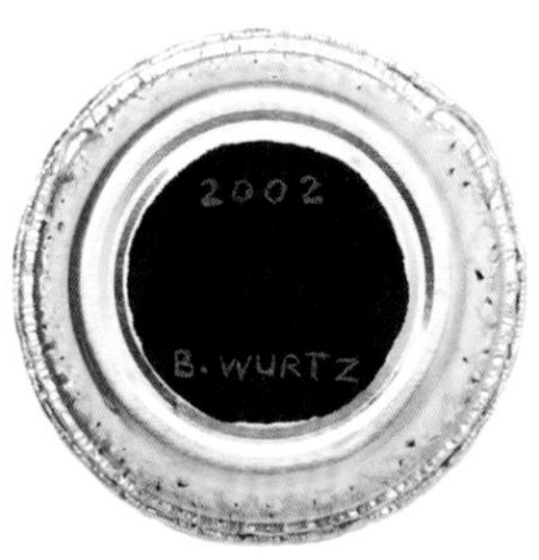

2002
B. WURTZ

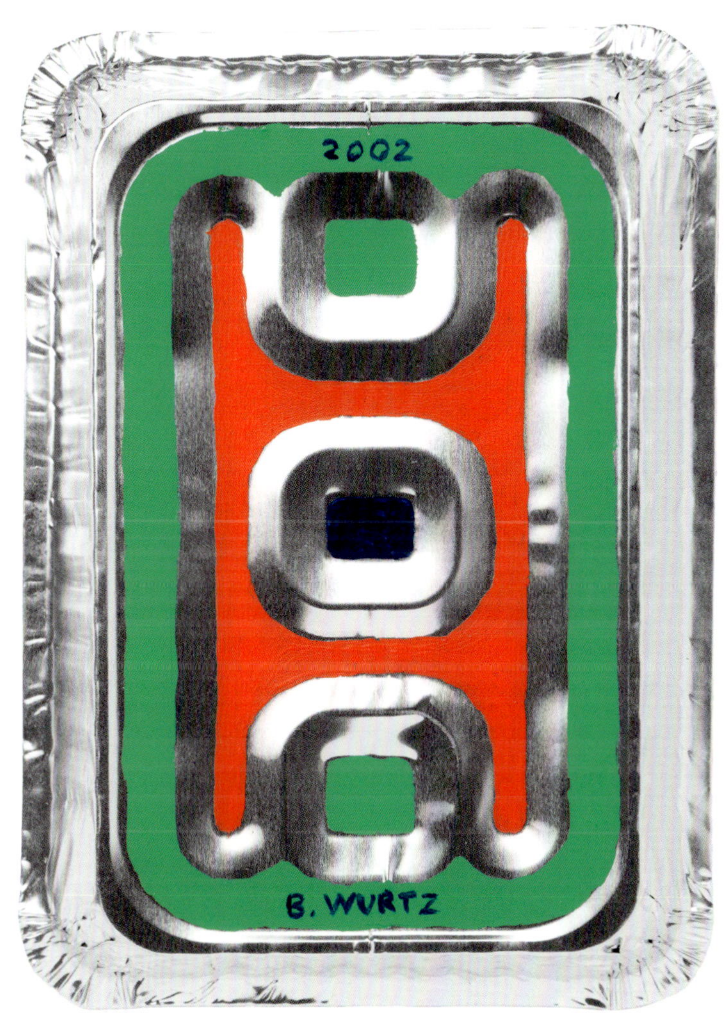

2002
B. WURTZ

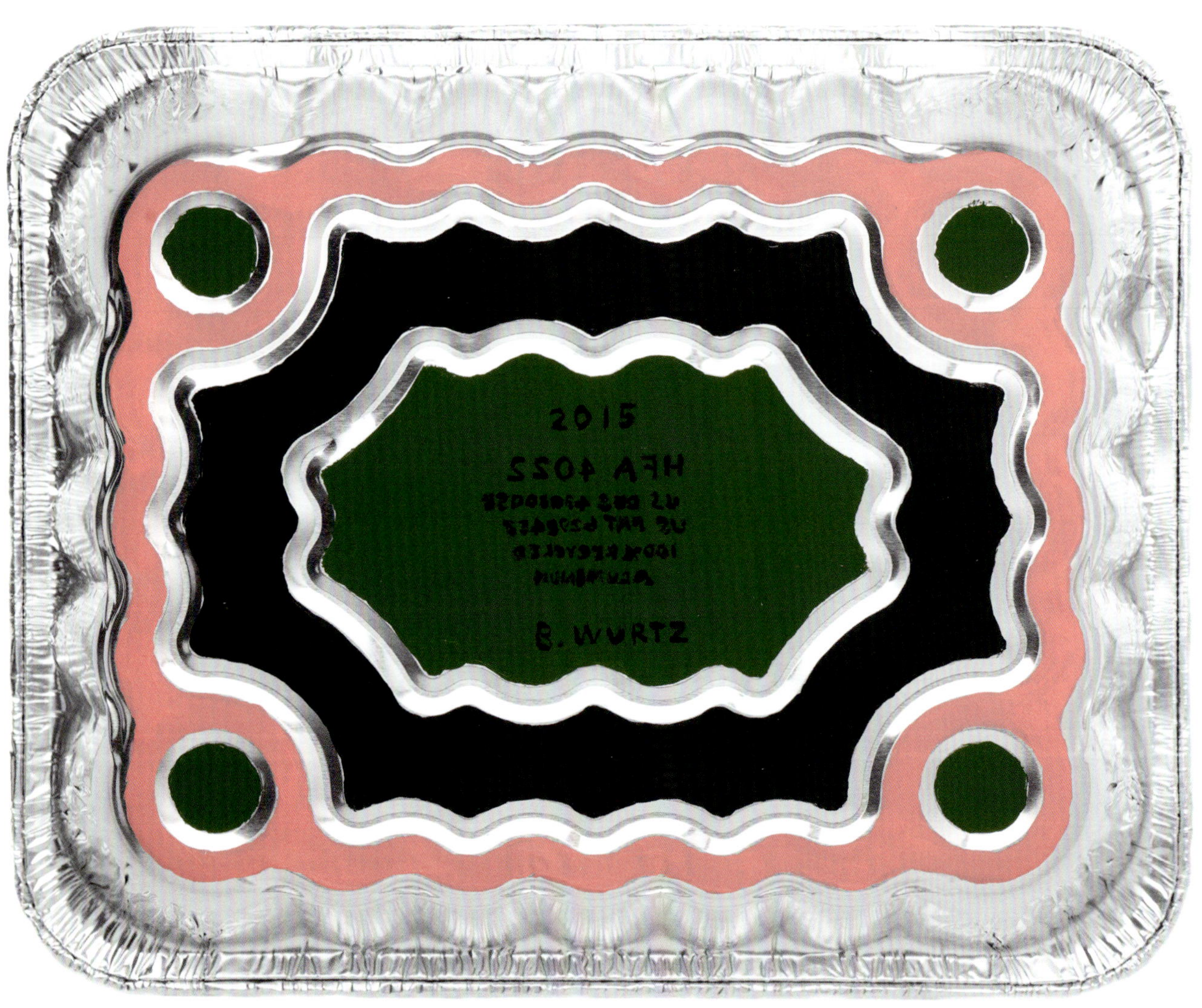
2015
HFA 4022
B.WURTZ

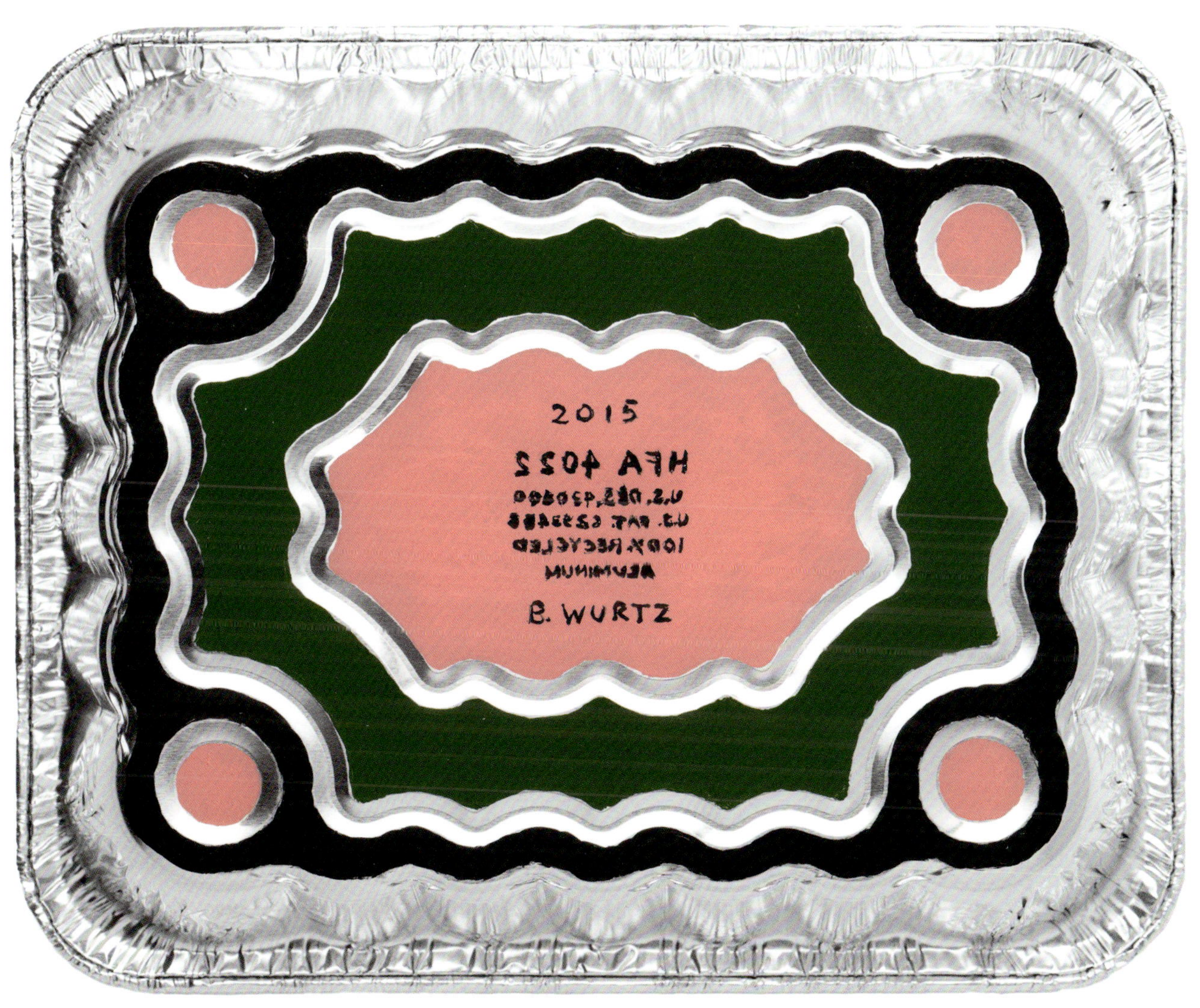
2015
HFA 4022
B. WURTZ

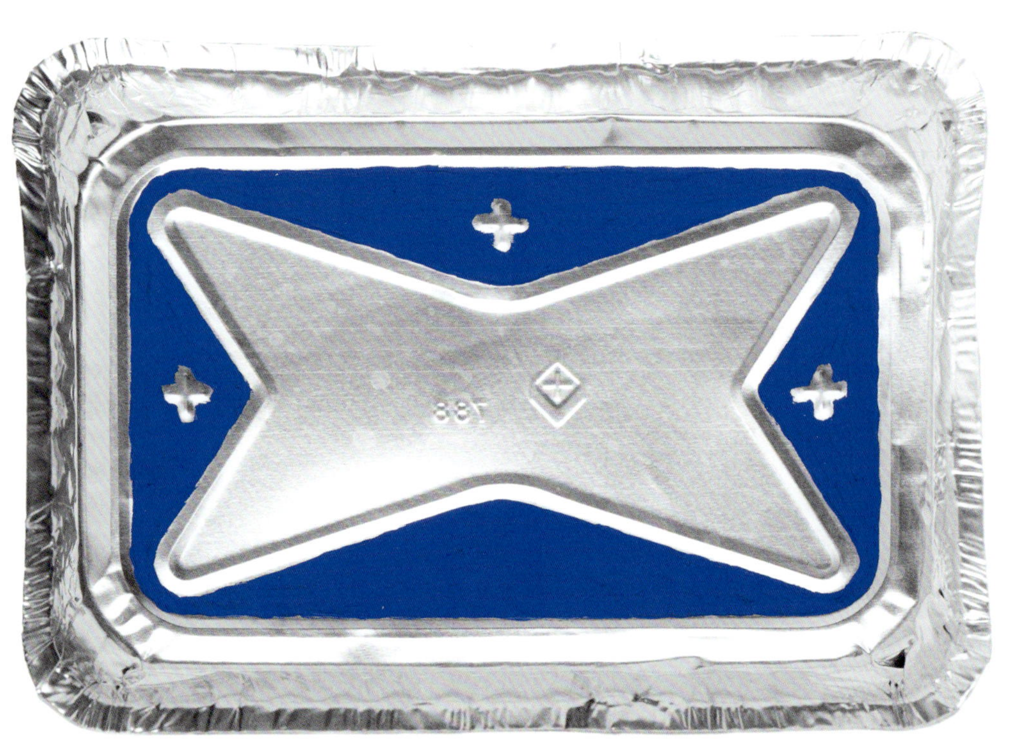

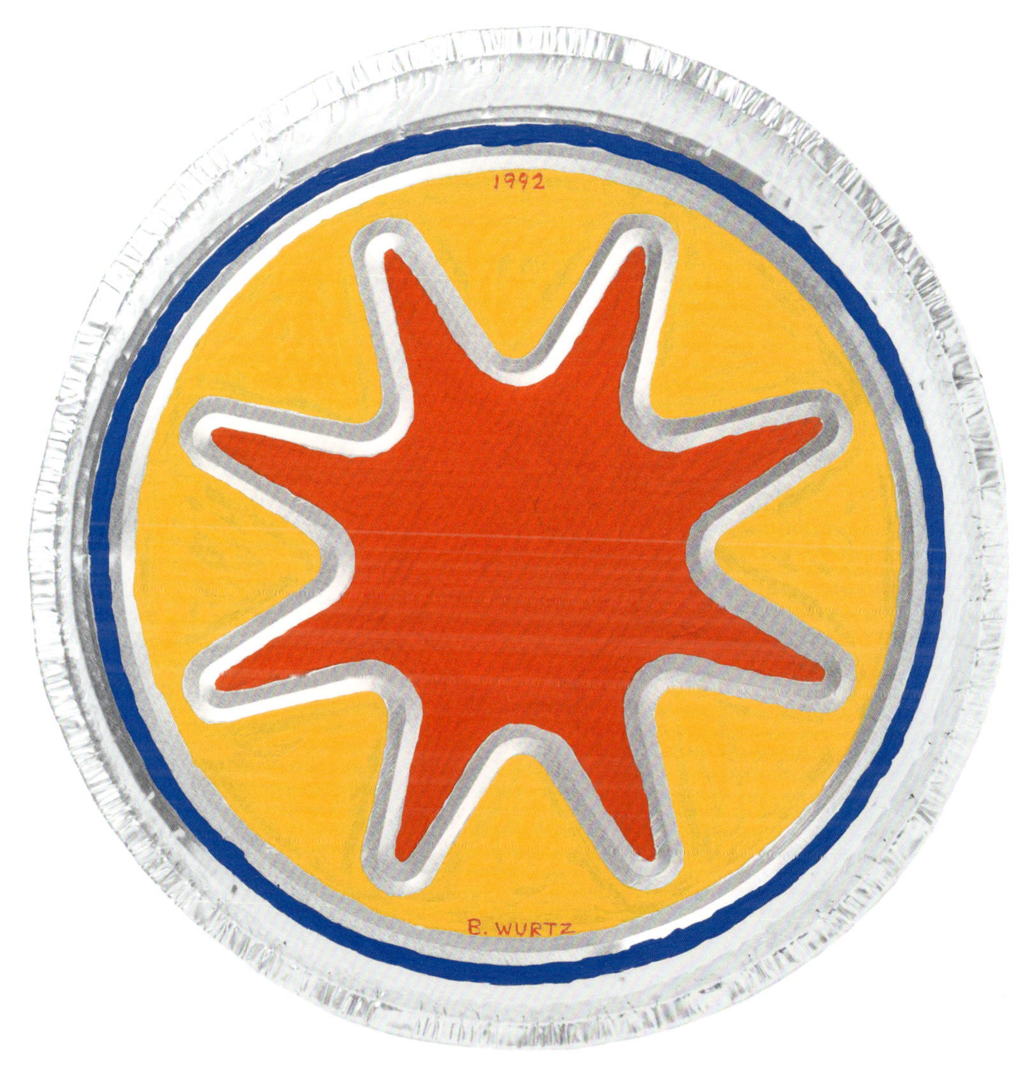

1992
B. WURTZ

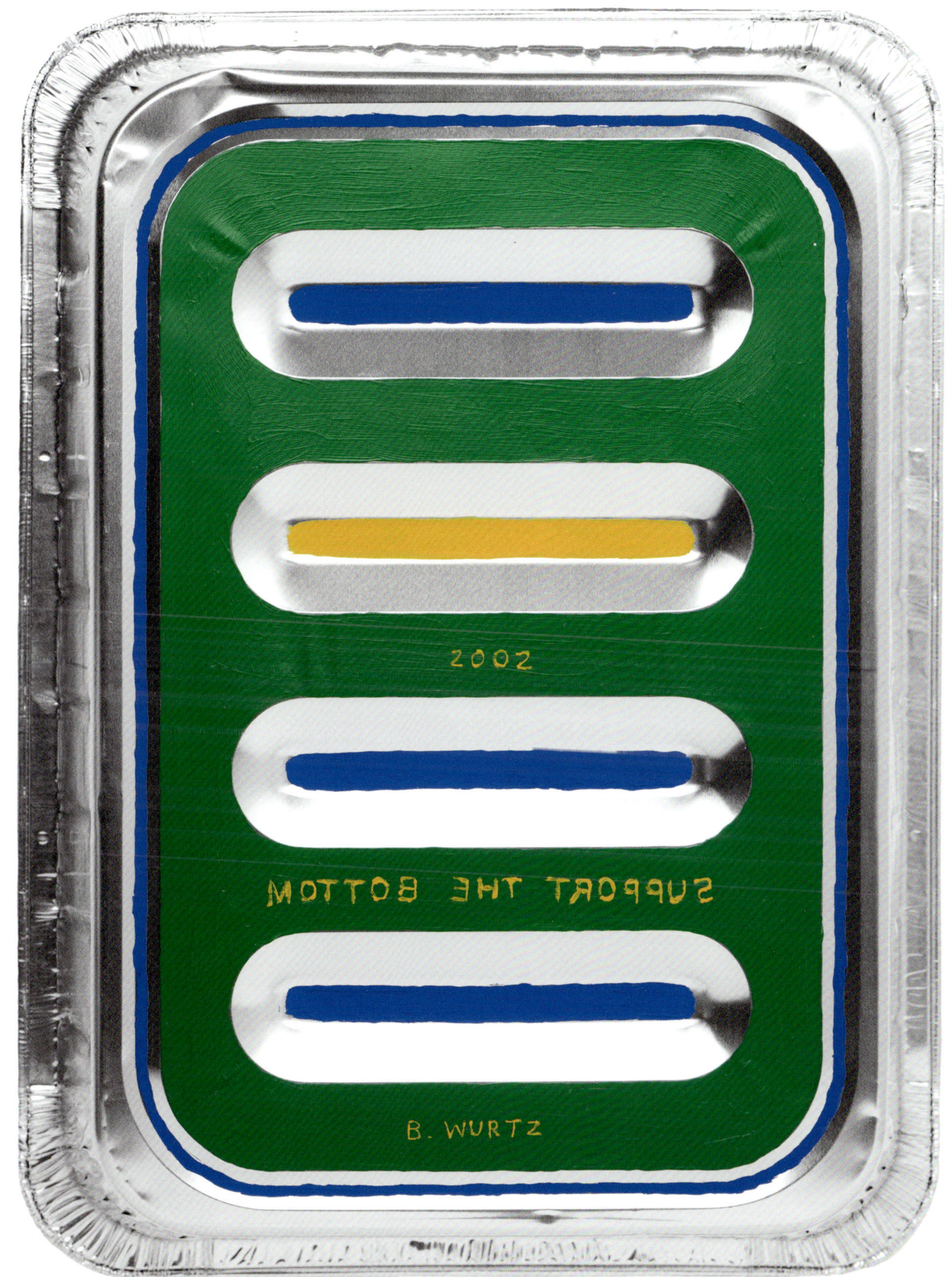
2002
SUPPORT THE BOTTOM
B. WURTZ

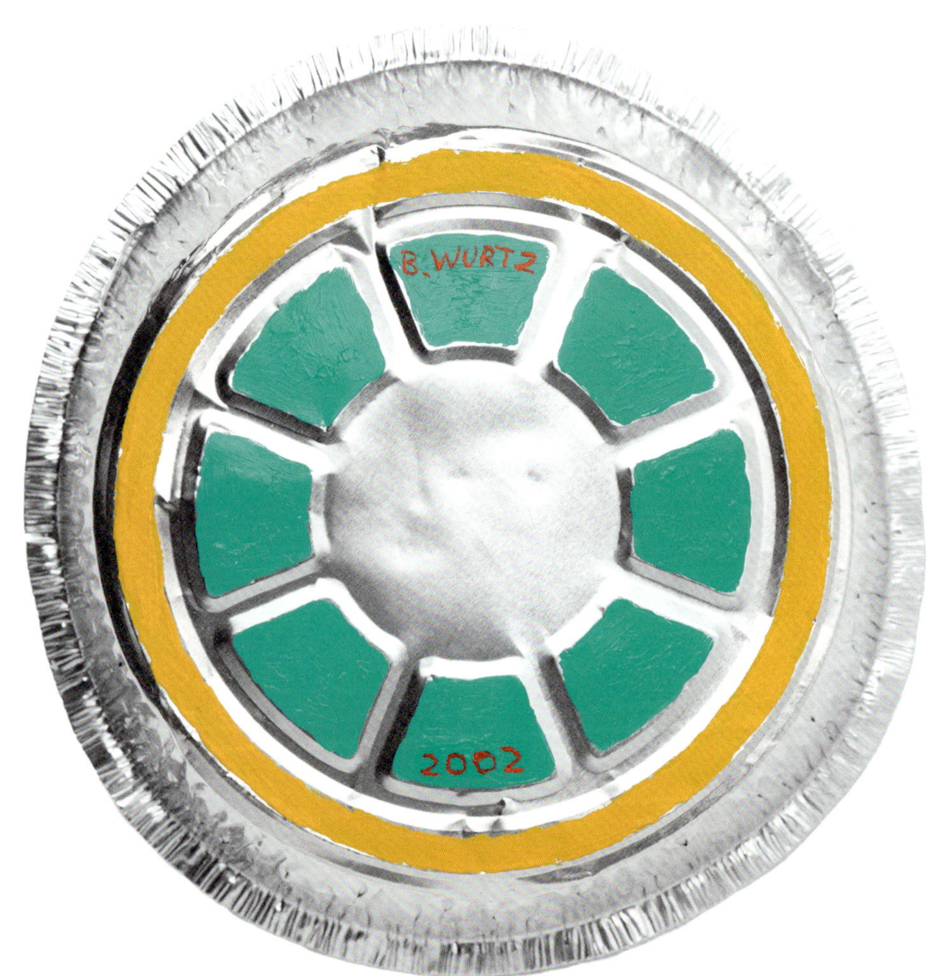
B. WURTZ
2002

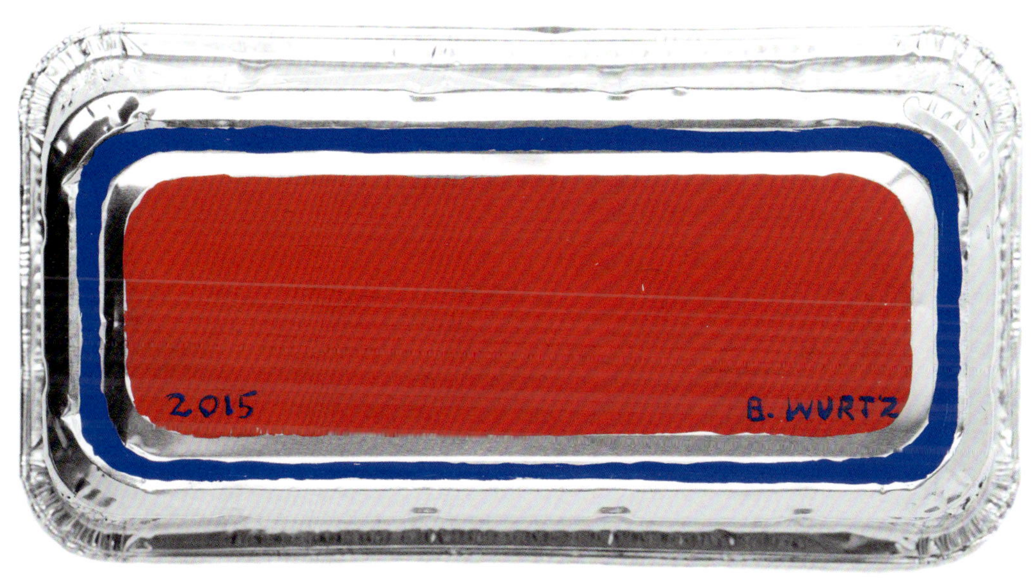

2015
B. WURTZ

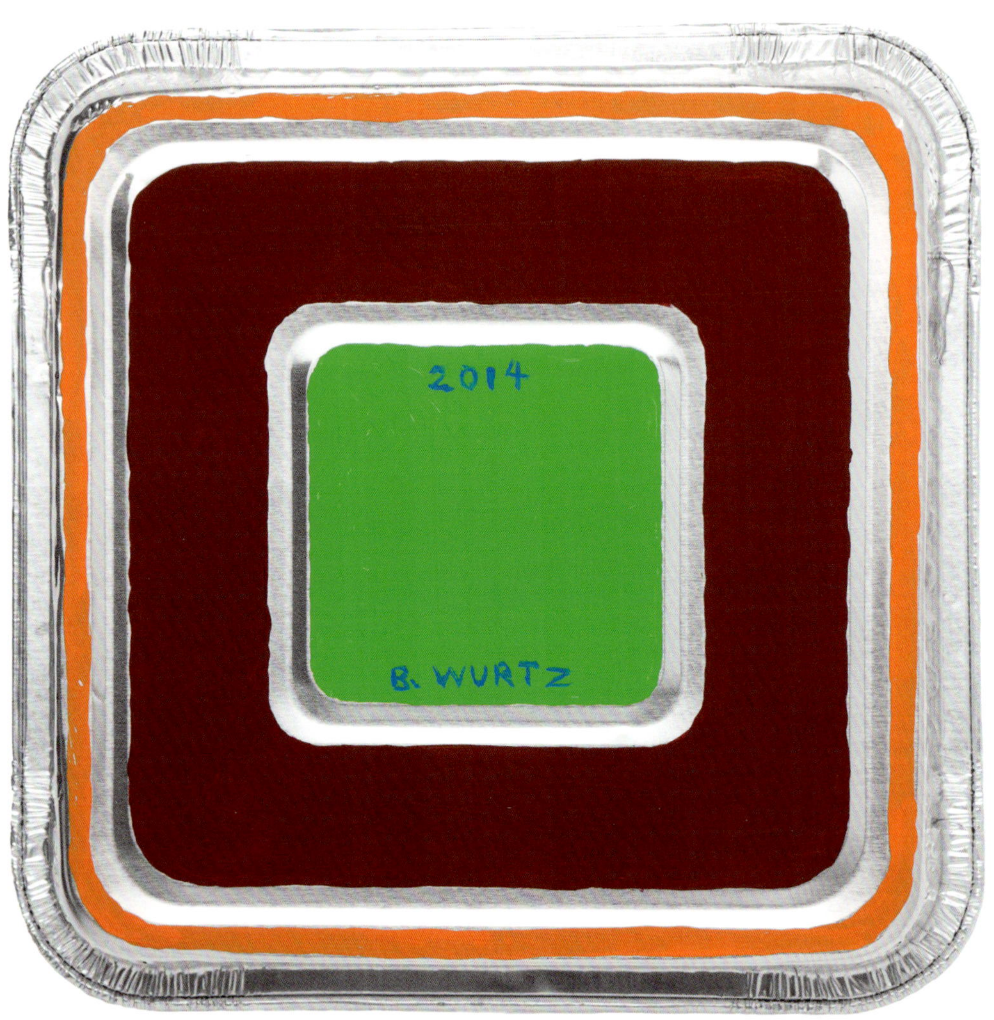

2014
B. WURTZ

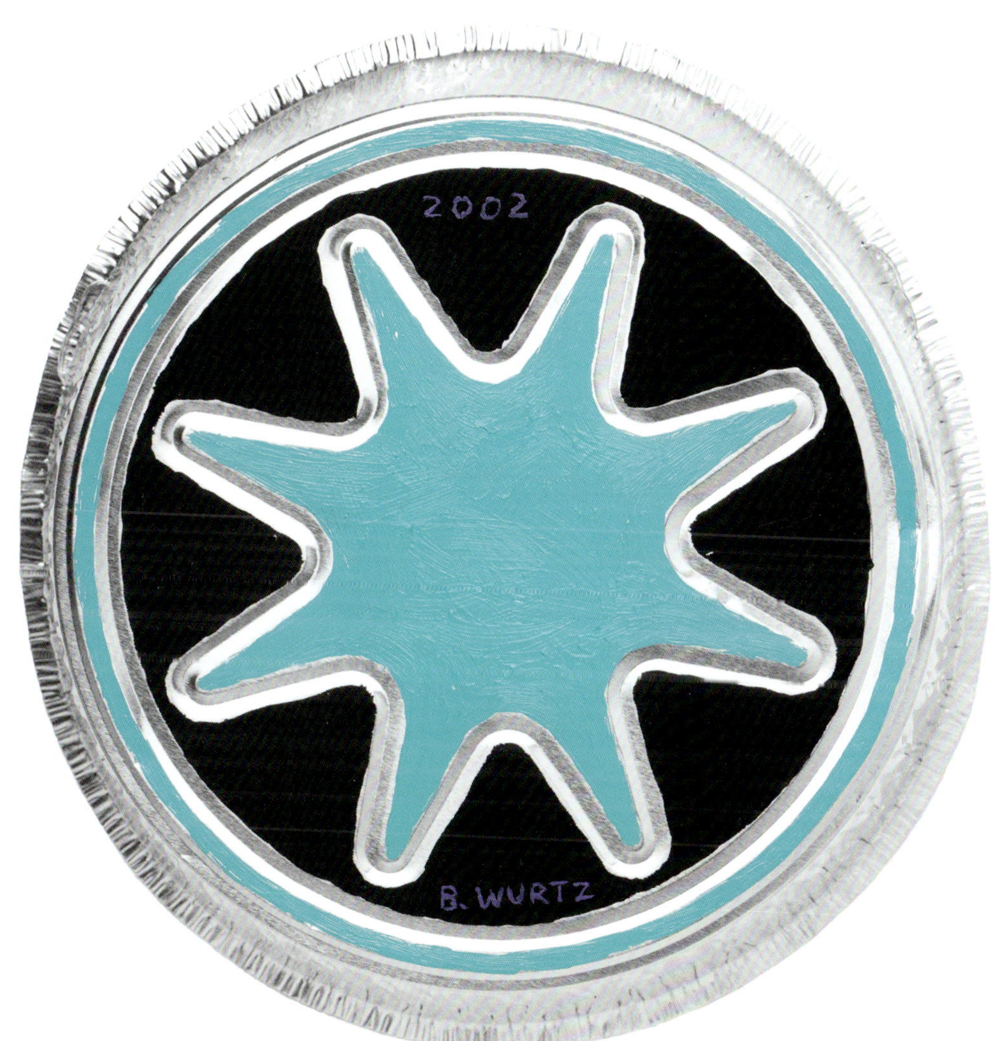
2002
B. WURTZ

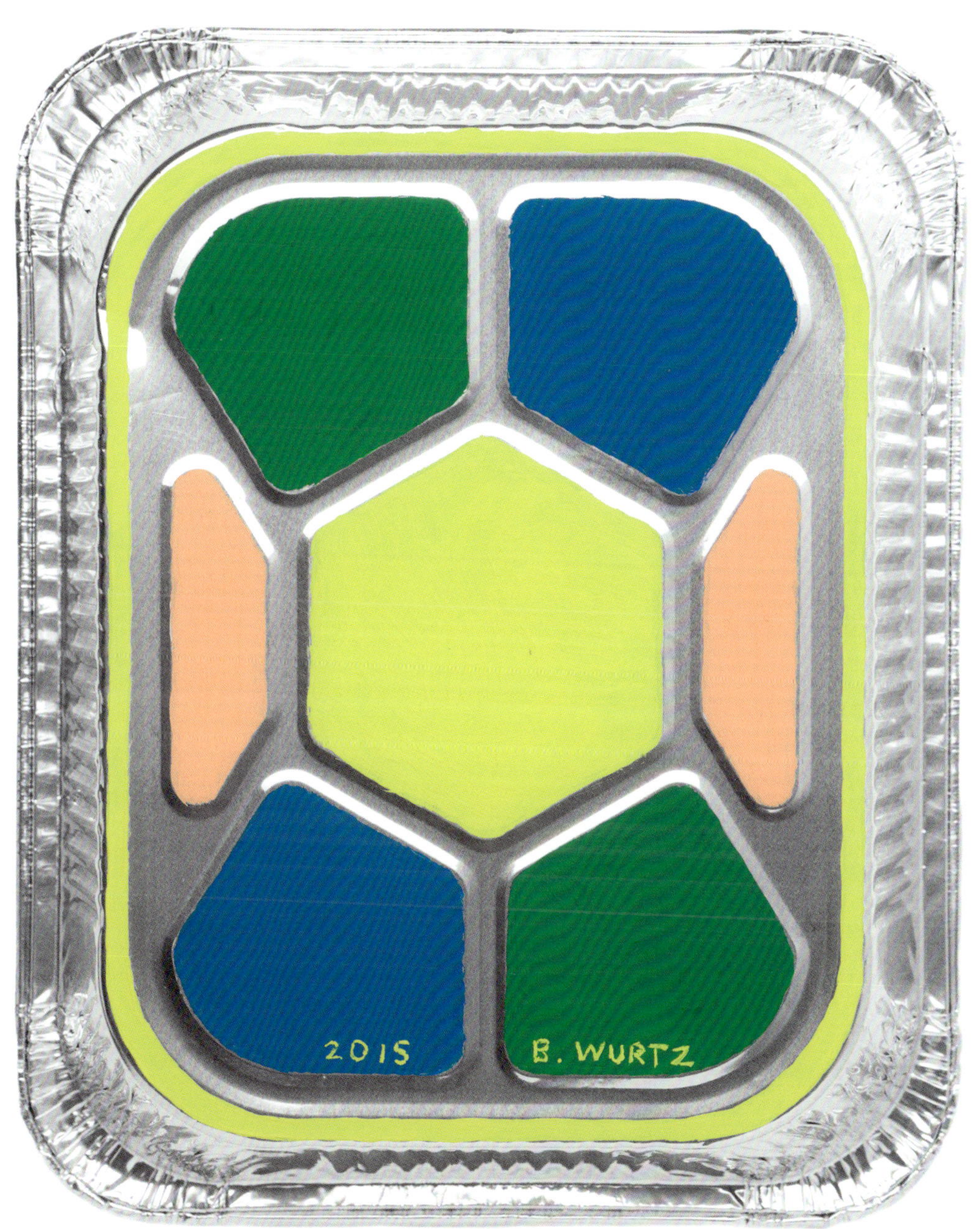
2015
B. WURTZ

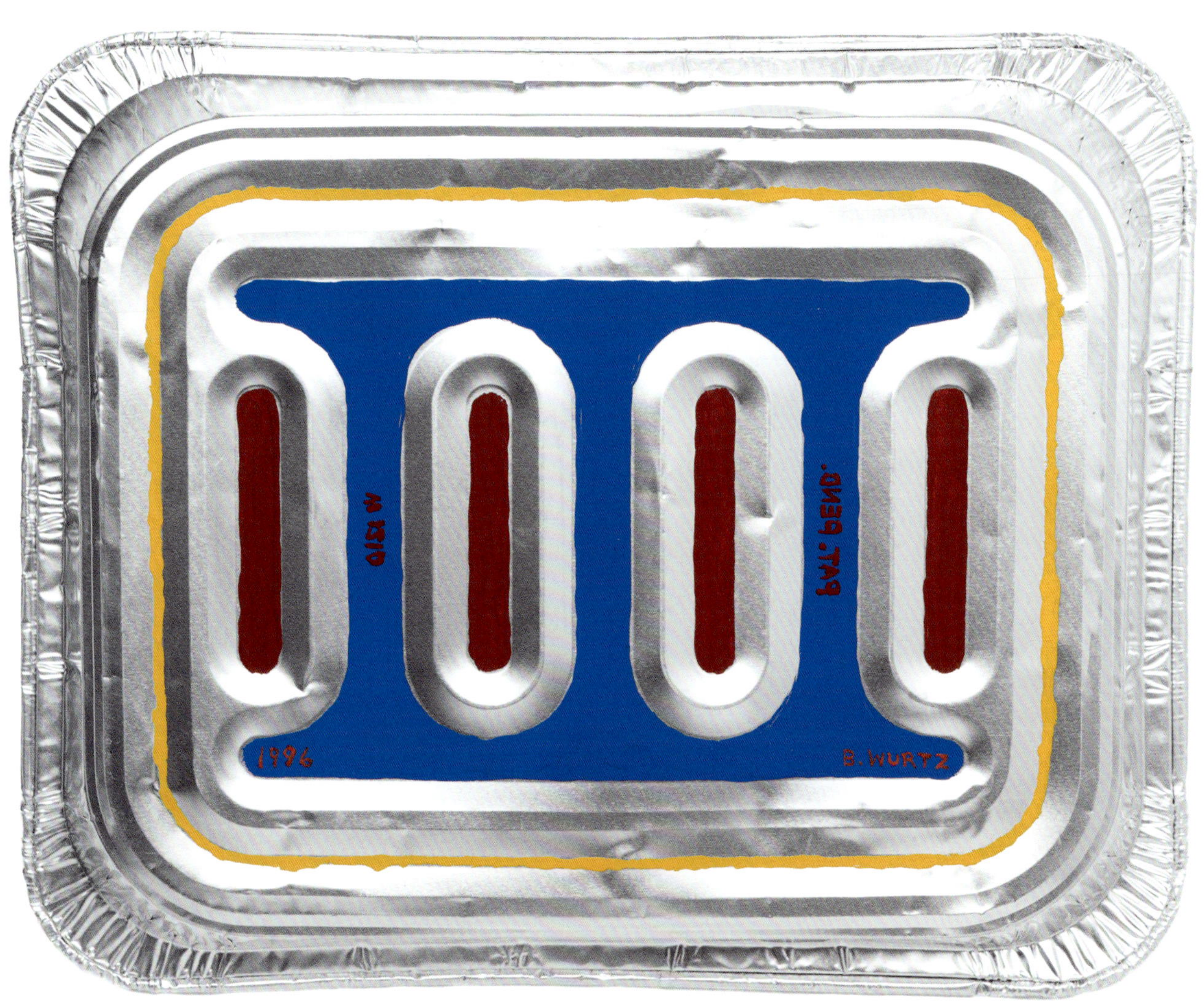
A KID
1996
PAT. PEND.
B.WURTZ

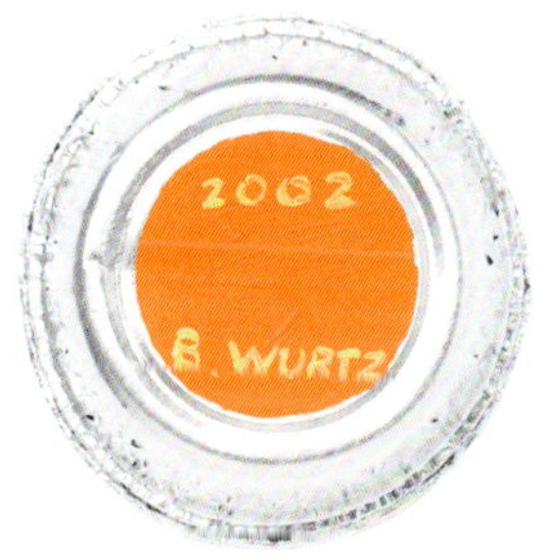
2002
B. WURTZ

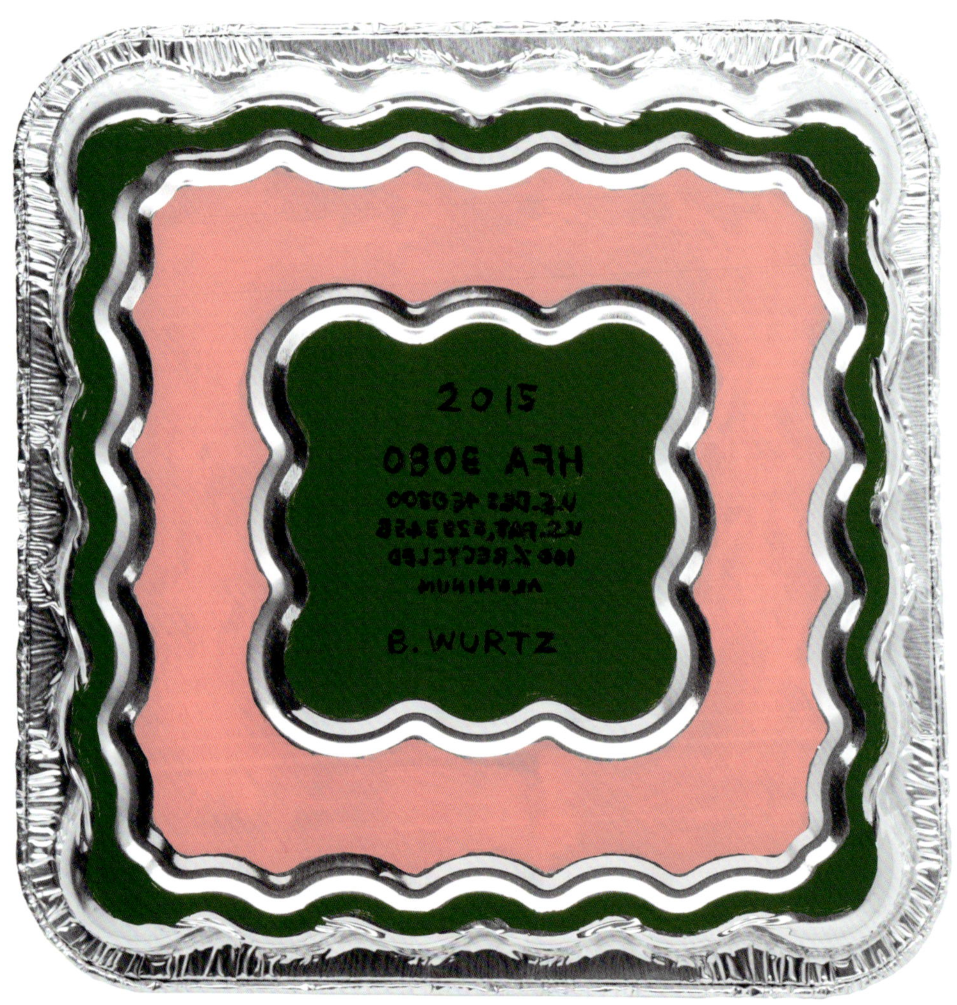

2015

HFA 3080
U.S. DES 460300
U.S. PAT. 8,293,458
100% RECYCLED
aluminum

B.WURTZ

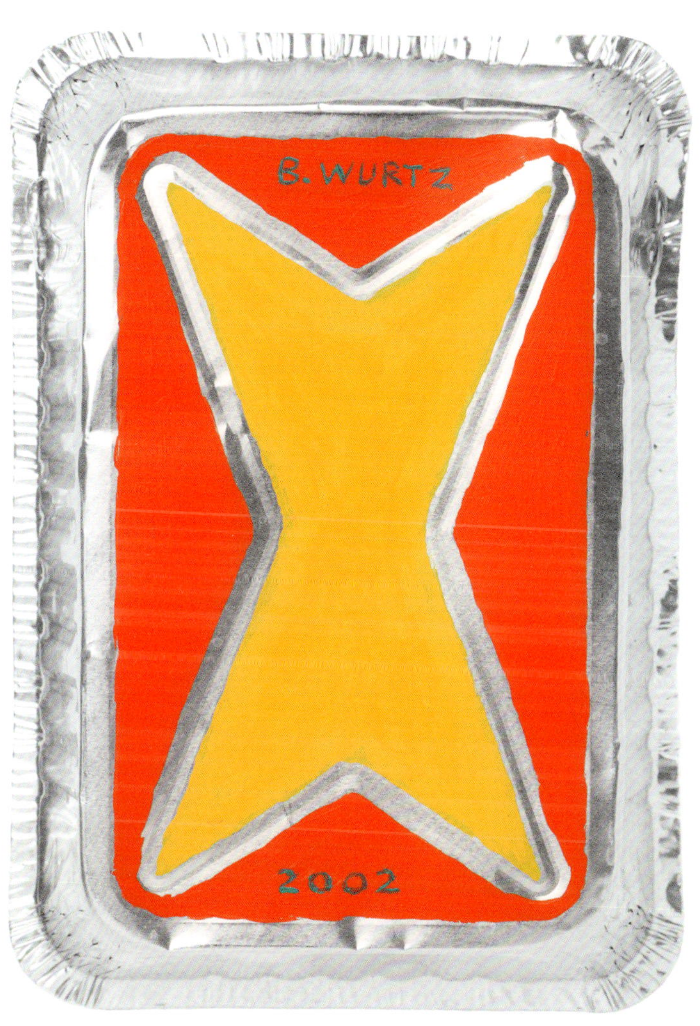
B. WURTZ
2002

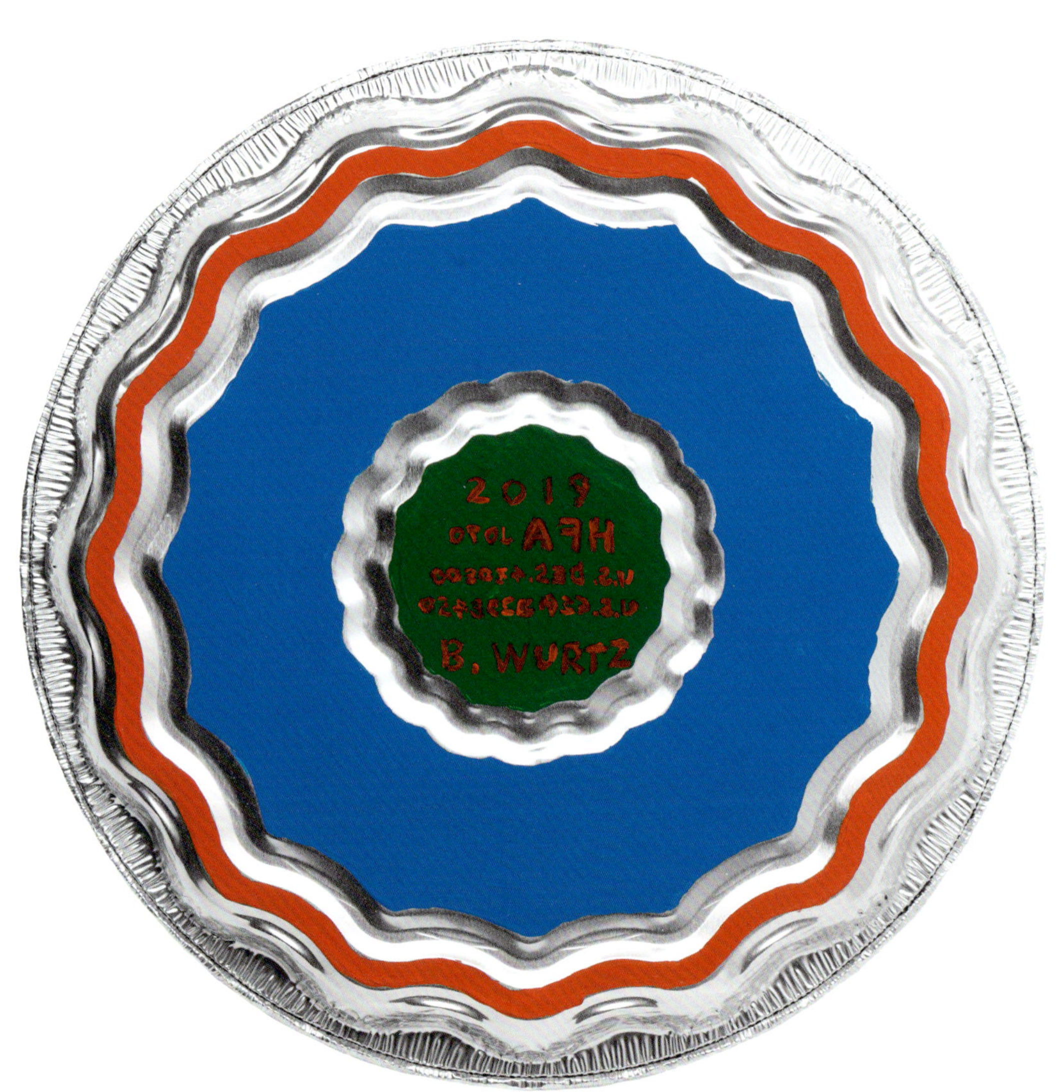
2019
HFA 1010
U.S. DES. 522,809
U.S.D 2,433,820
B. WURTZ

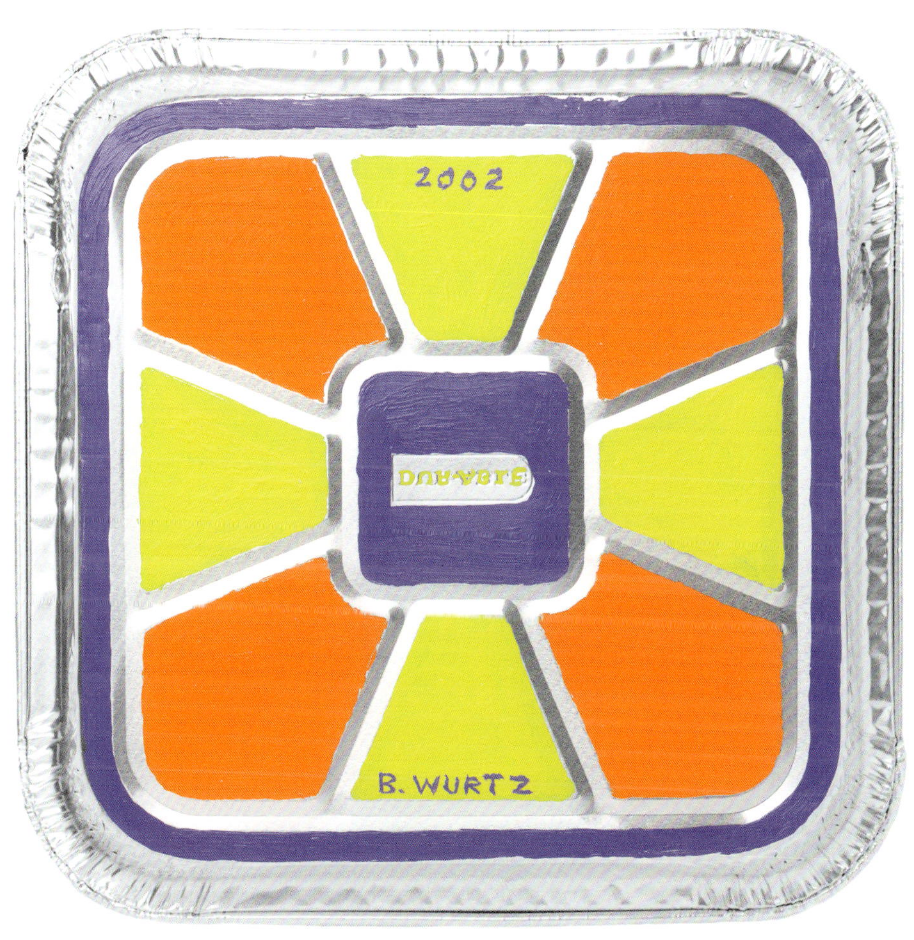

2002
B. WURTZ

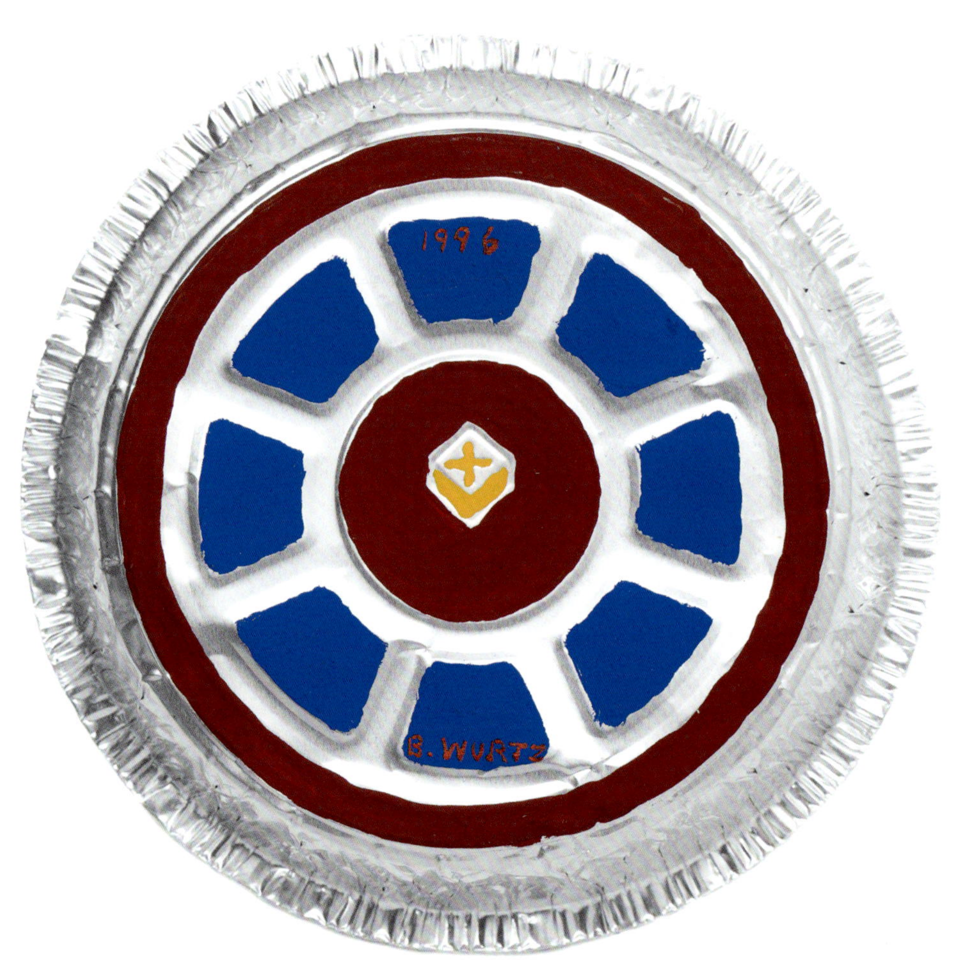

1996
G. WURTZ

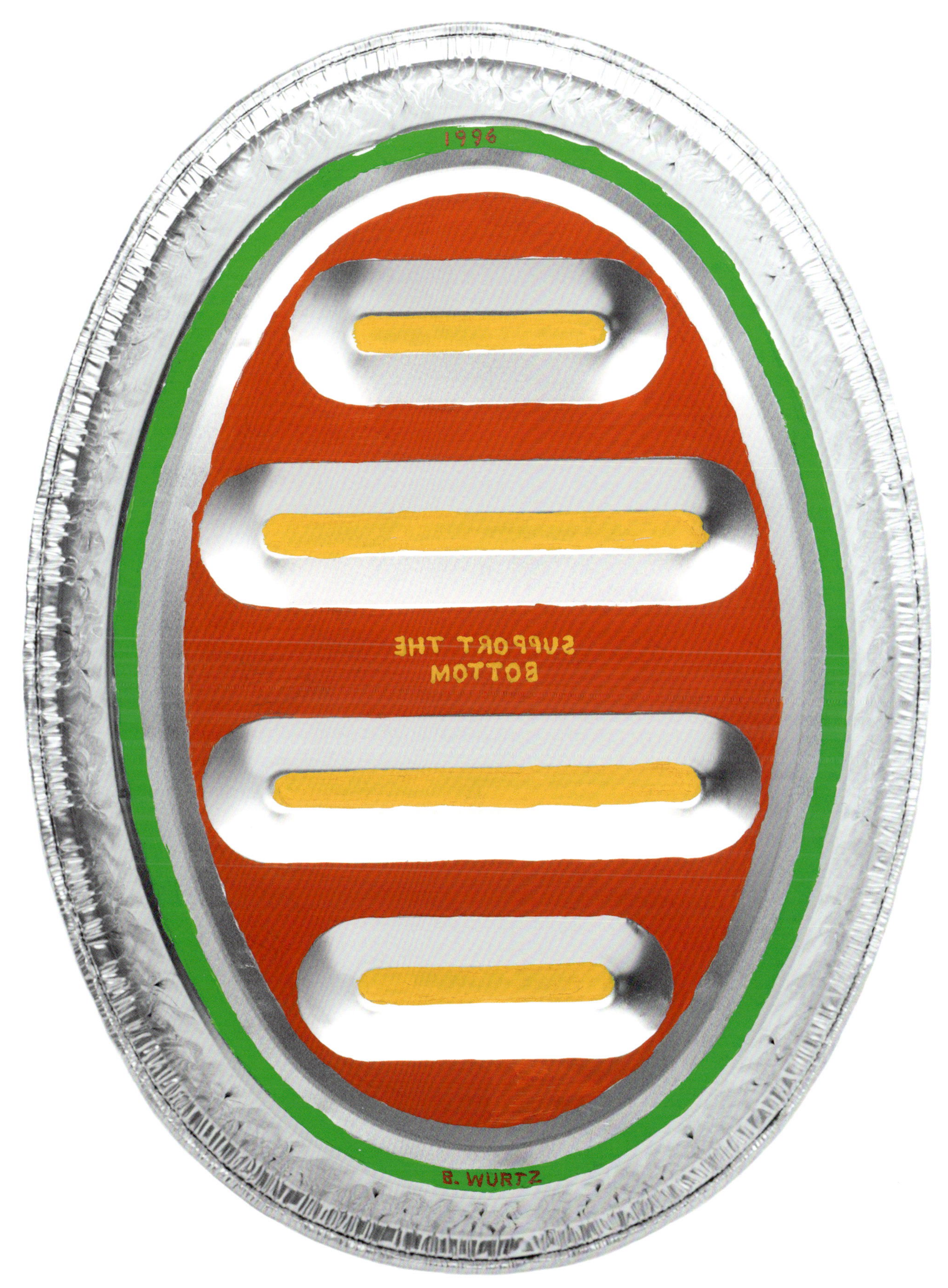
1996
SUPPORT THE
BOTTOM
B. WURTZ

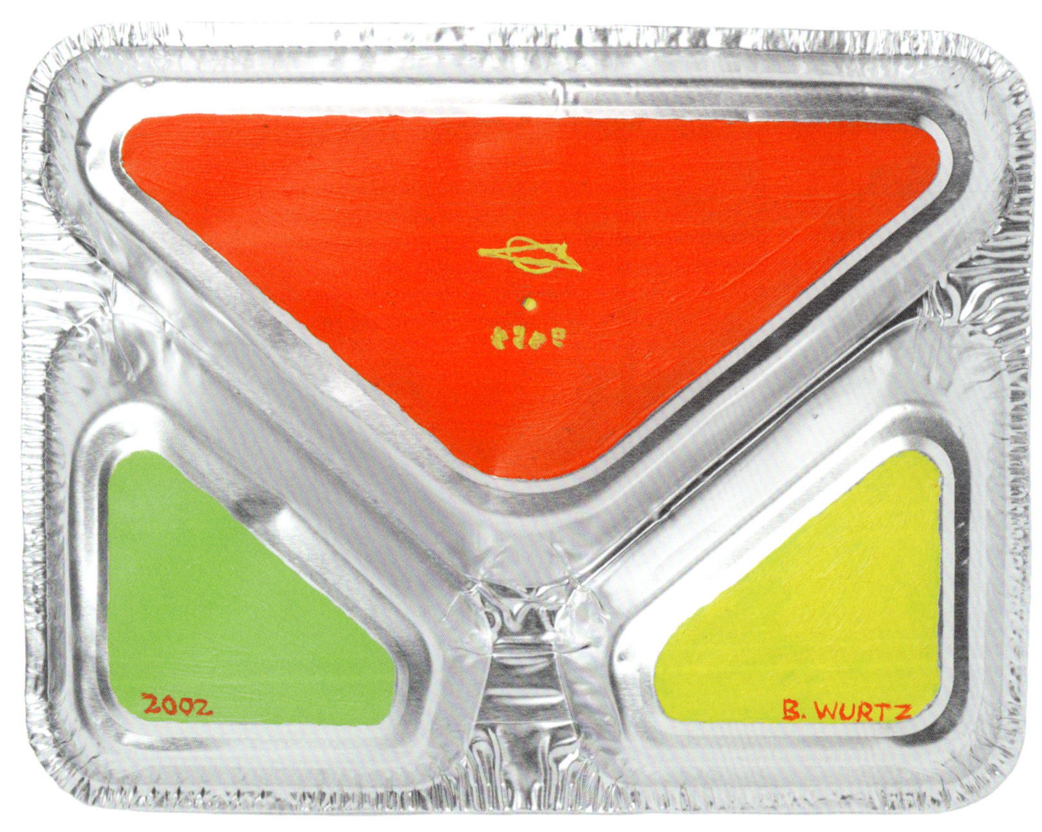

2002
B. WURTZ

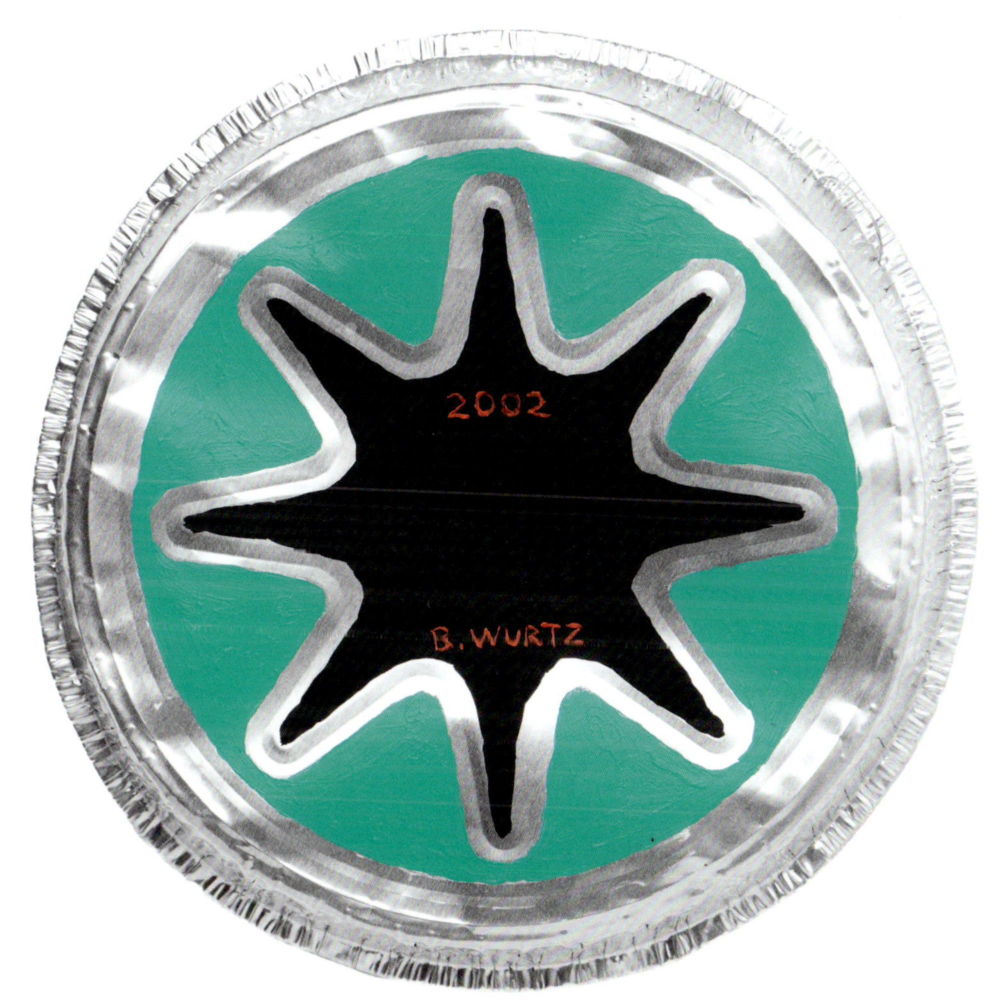
2002
B. WURTZ

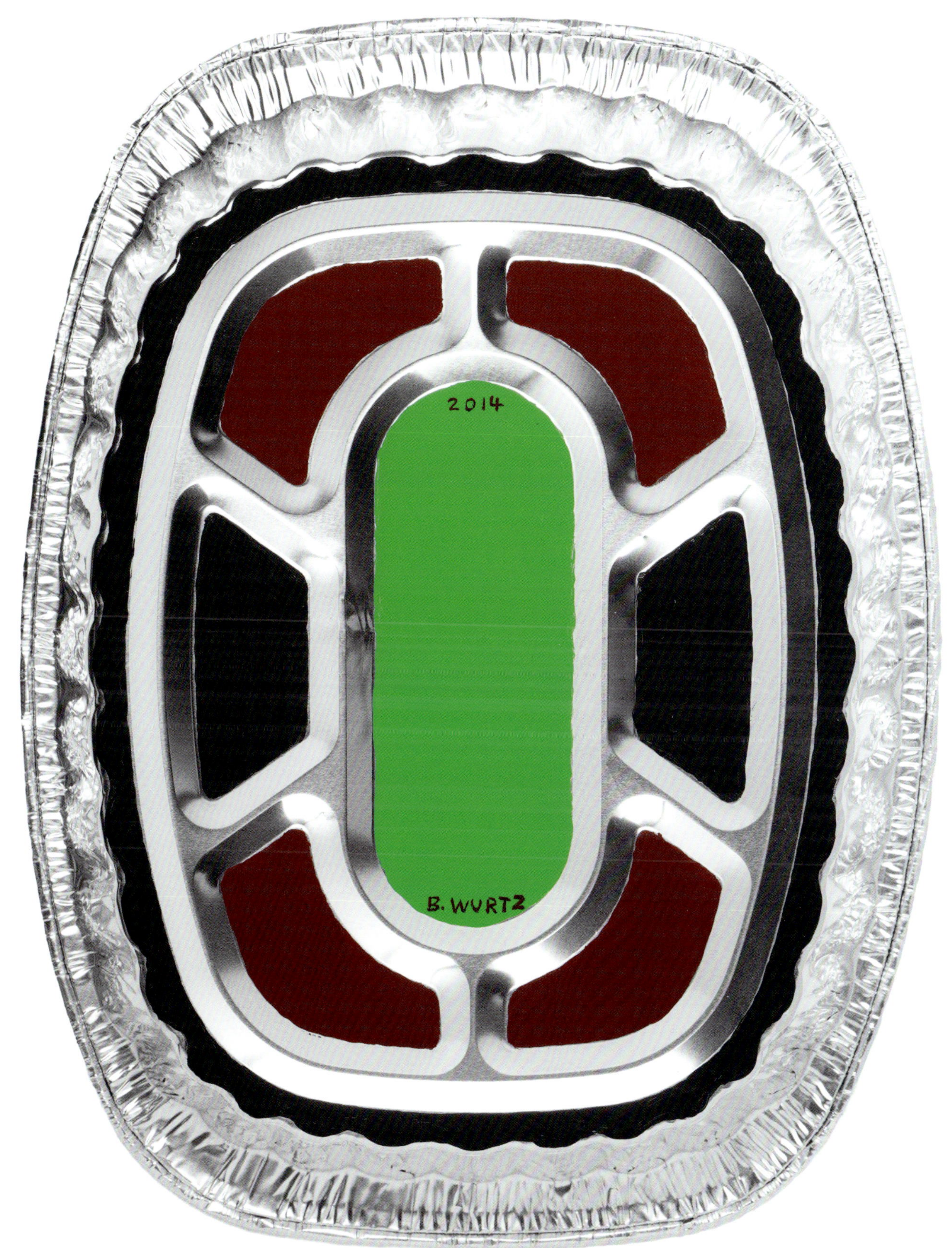

2014
B. WURTZ

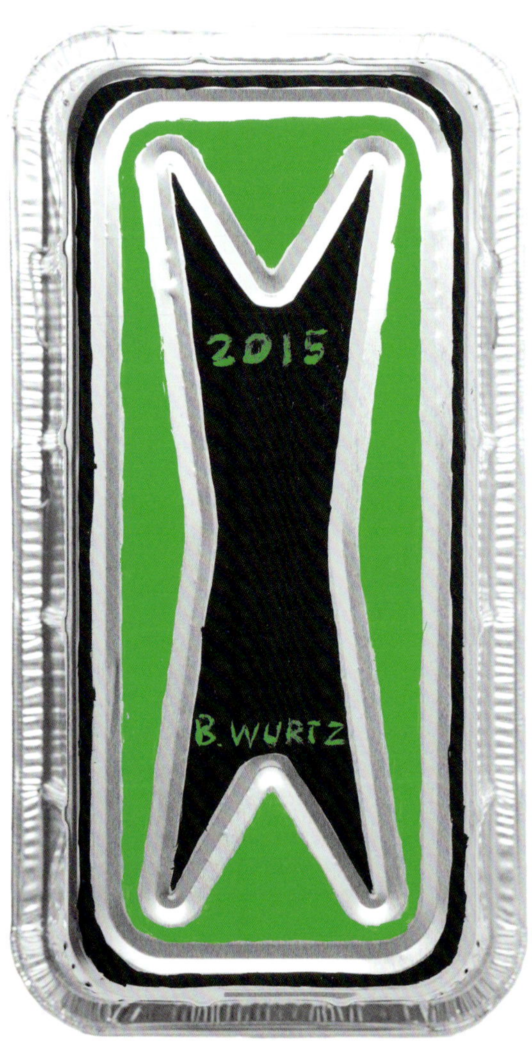
2015
B.WURTZ

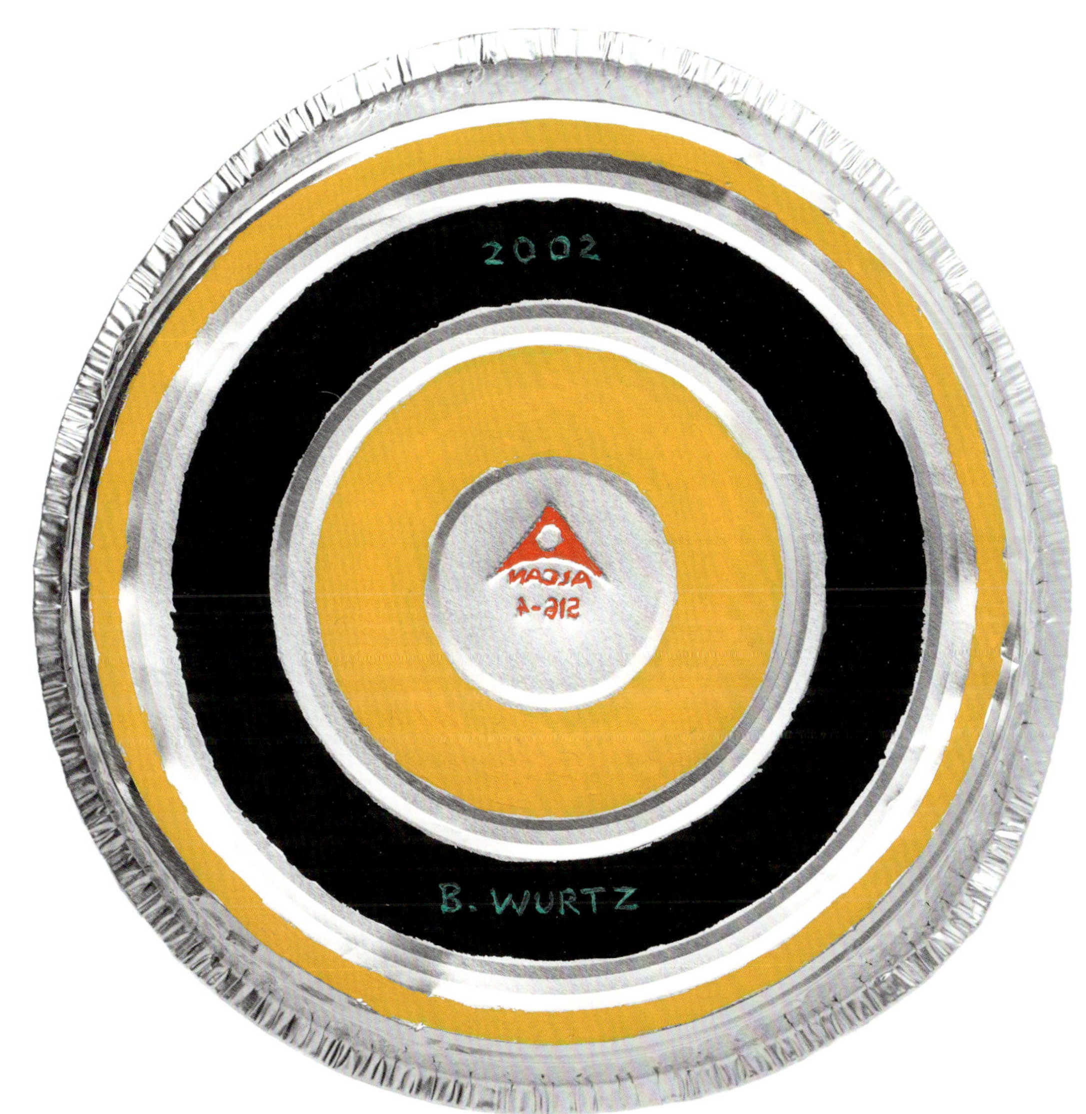
2002
B. WURTZ

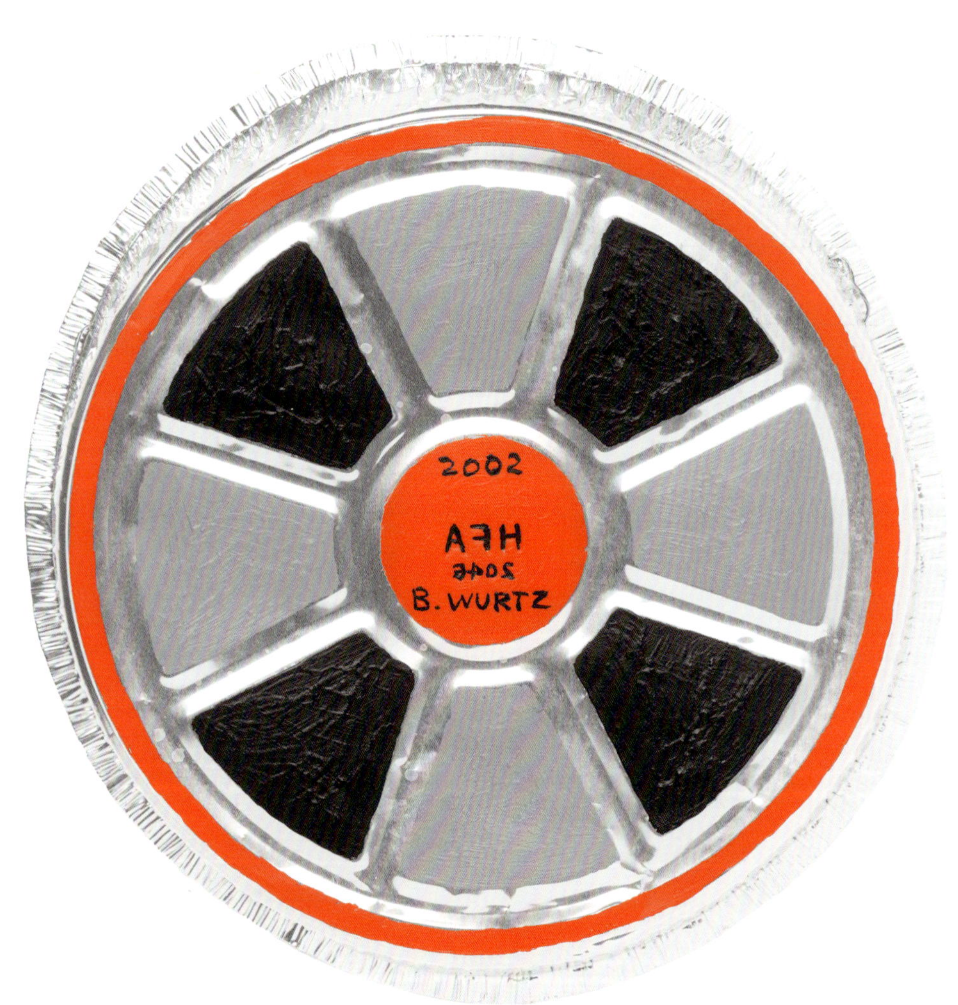

2002
AFH
2046
B. WURTZ

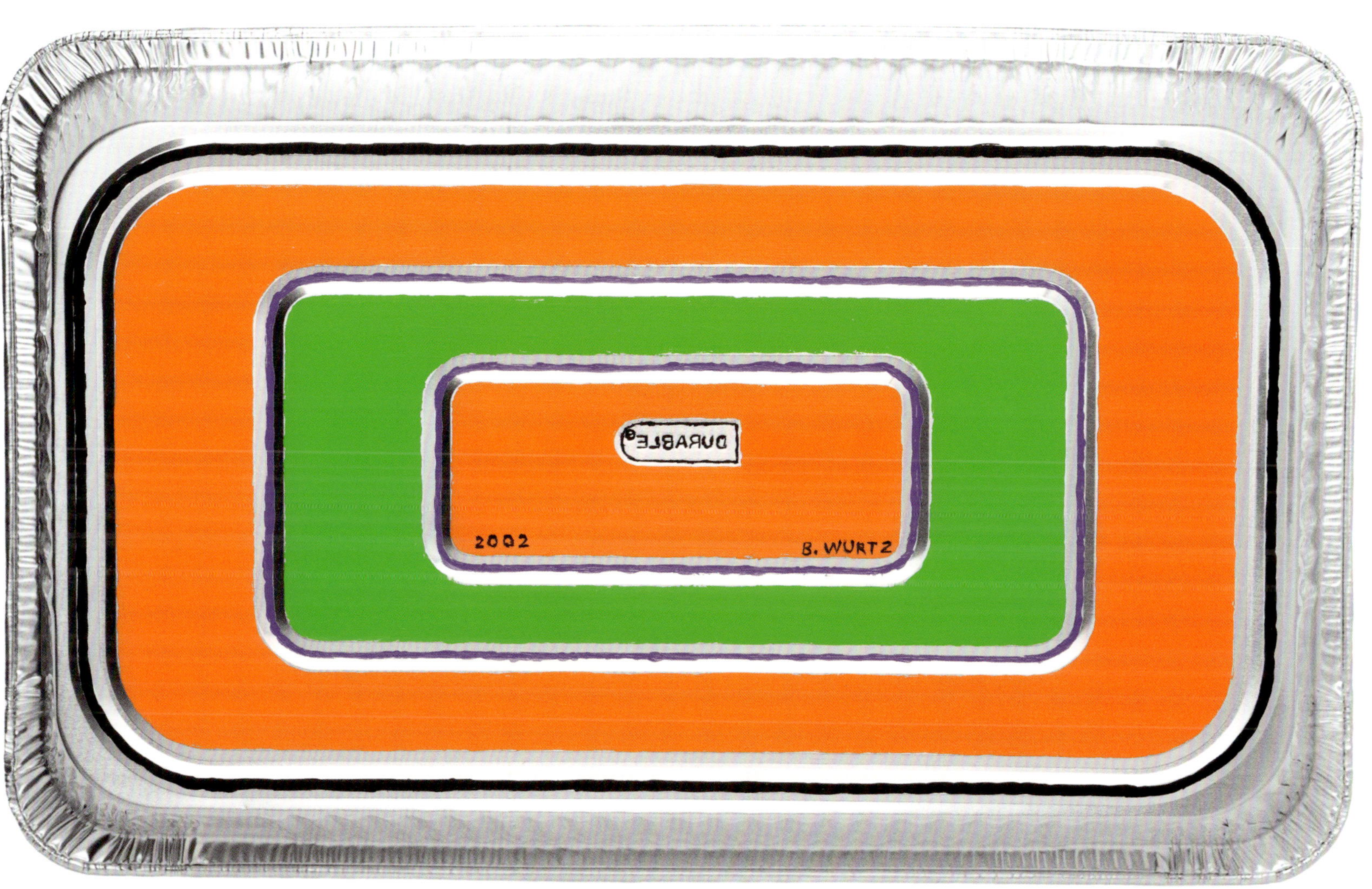
DURABLE
2002
B. WURTZ

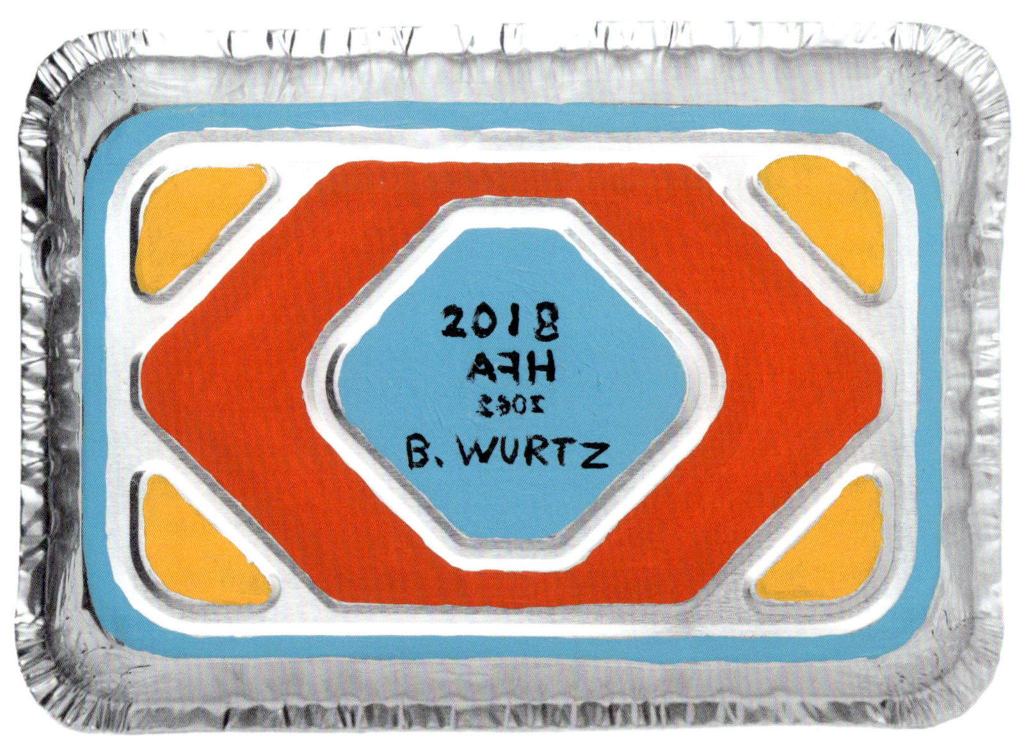
2018
AFH
2065
B. WURTZ

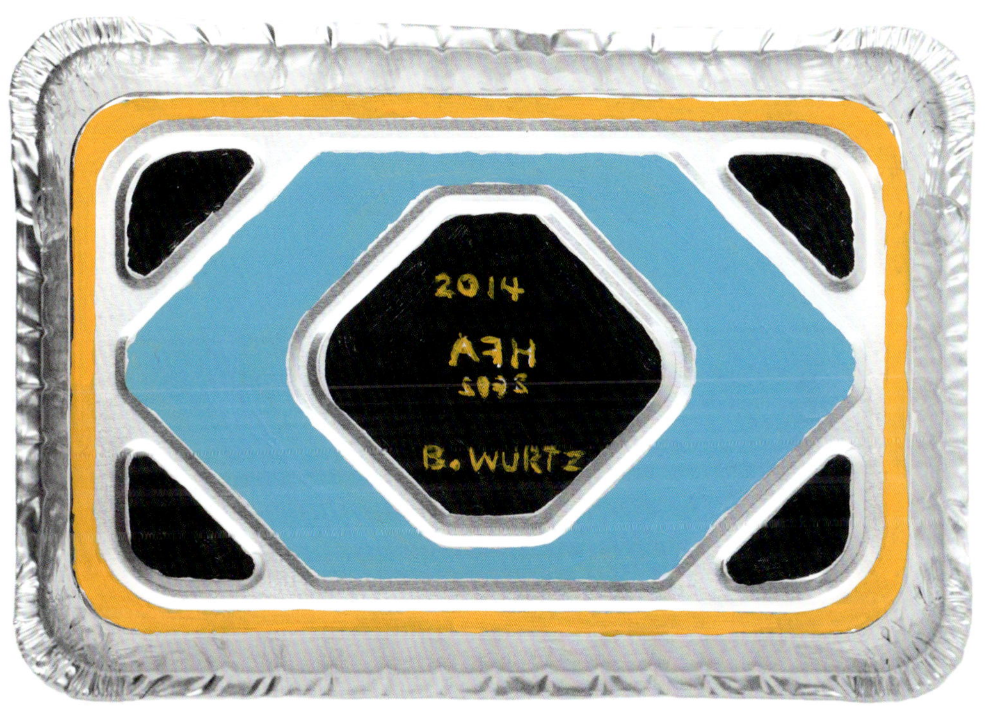

2014
AFH
2015
B. WURTZ

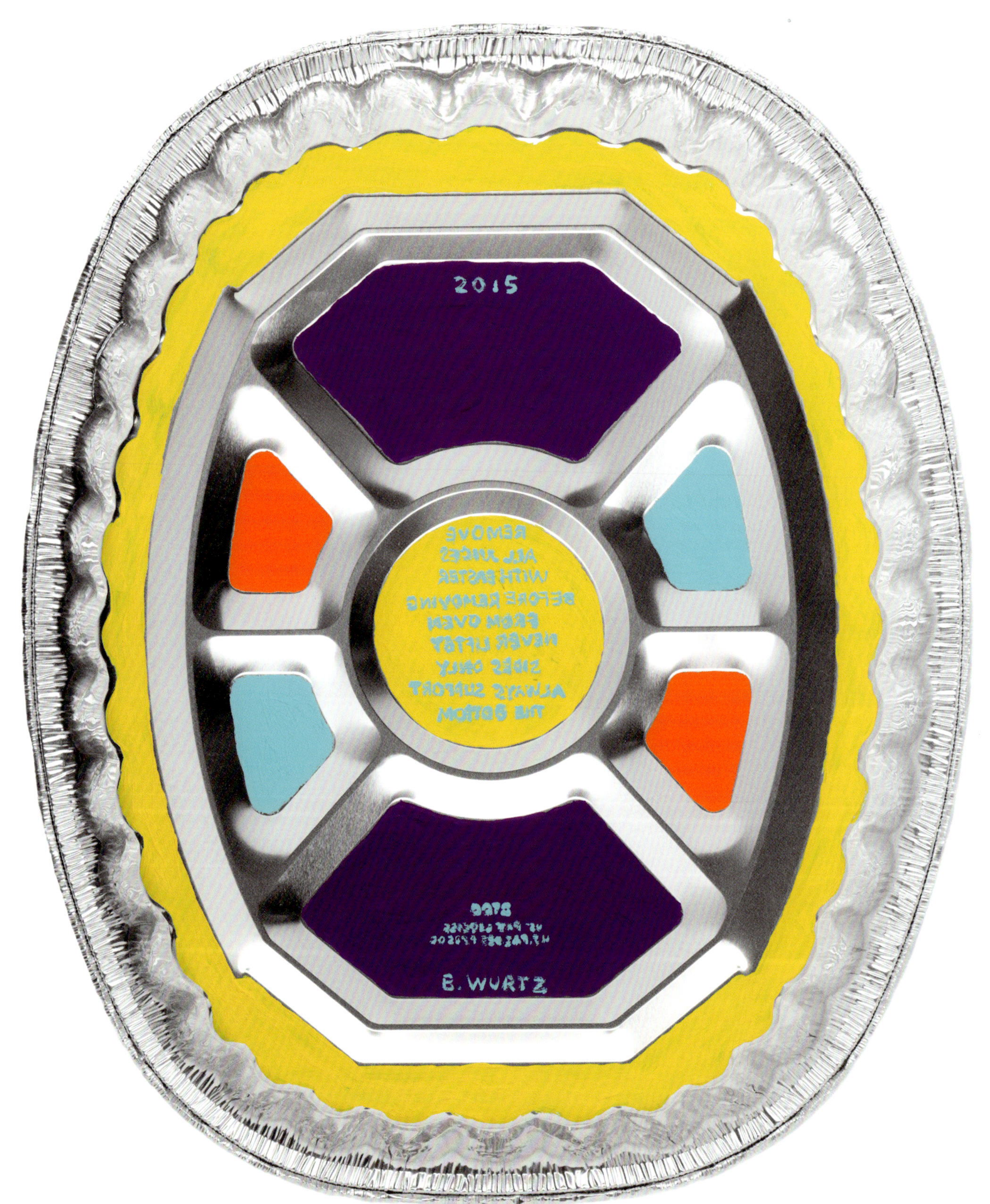

2015
REMOVE ALL JUICES WITH BASTER BEFORE REMOVING FROM OVEN NEVER LIFT SIDES ONLY ALWAYS SUPPORT THE BOTTOM
B. WURTZ

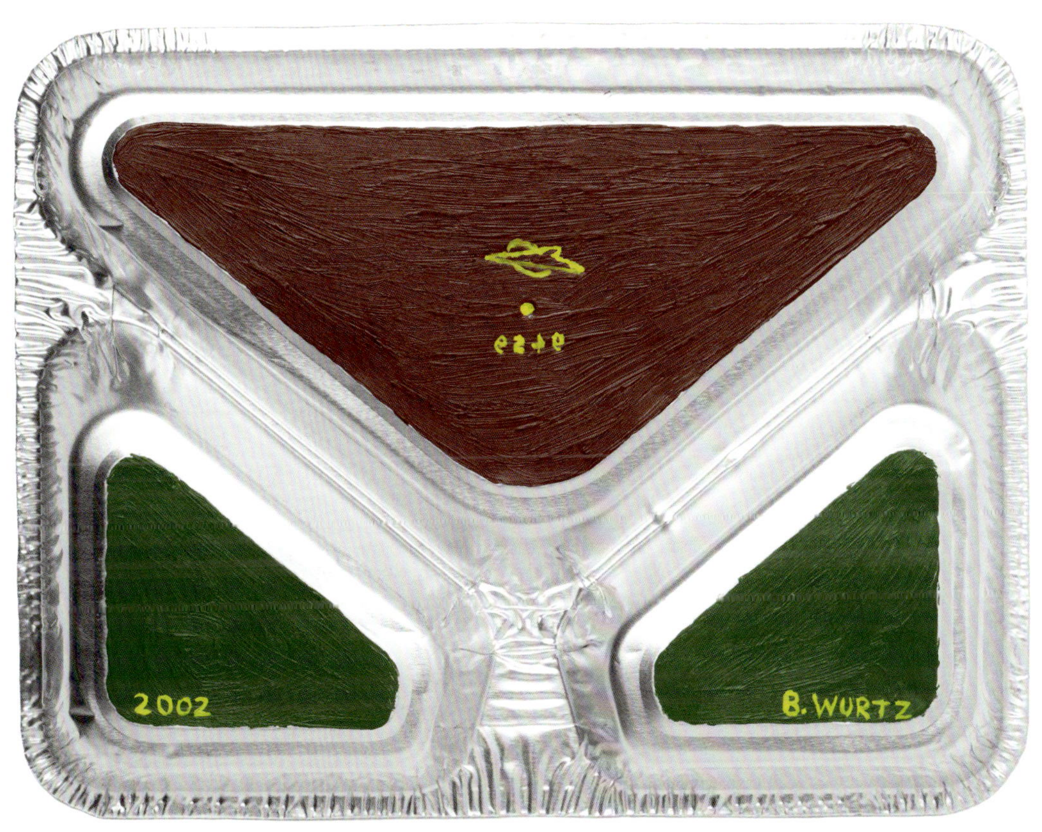

2002
B. WURTZ

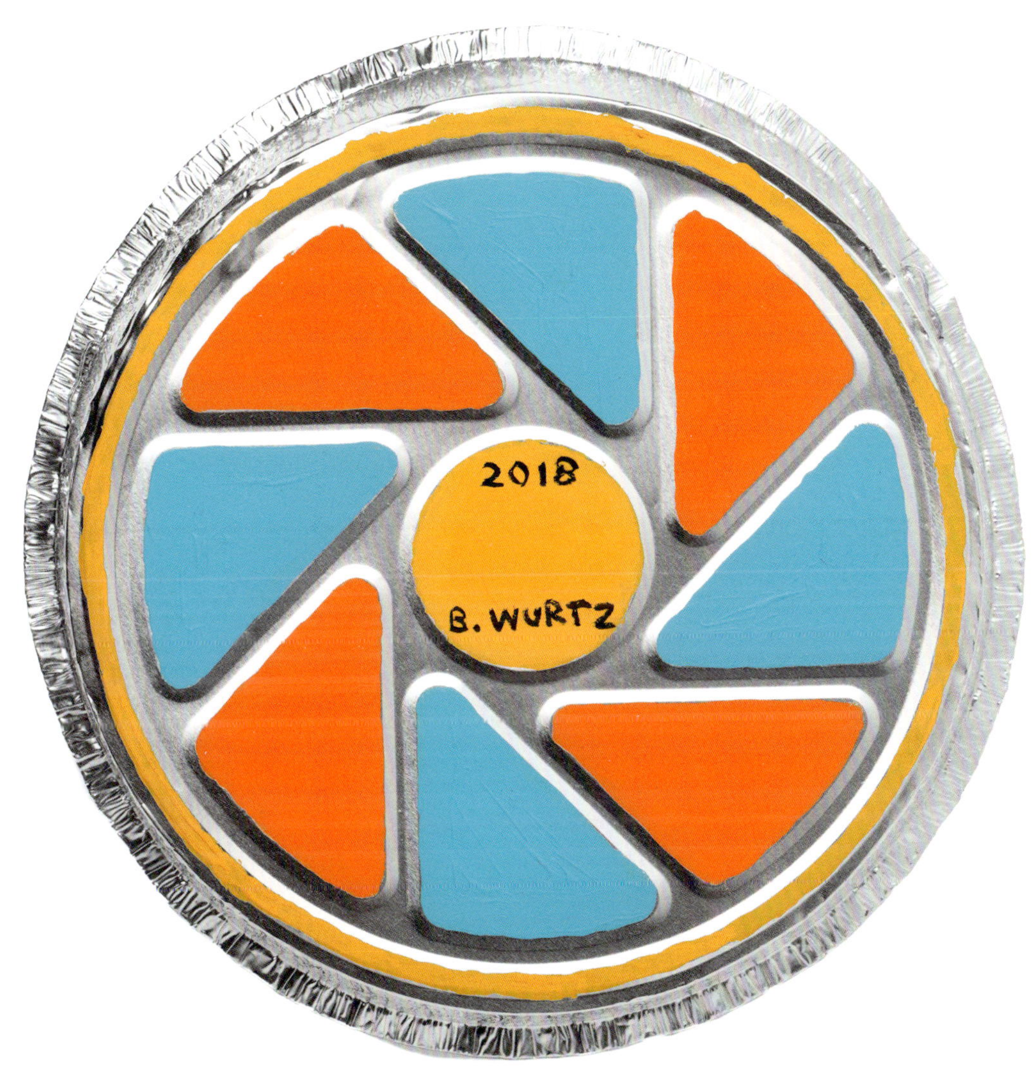

2018
B. WURTZ

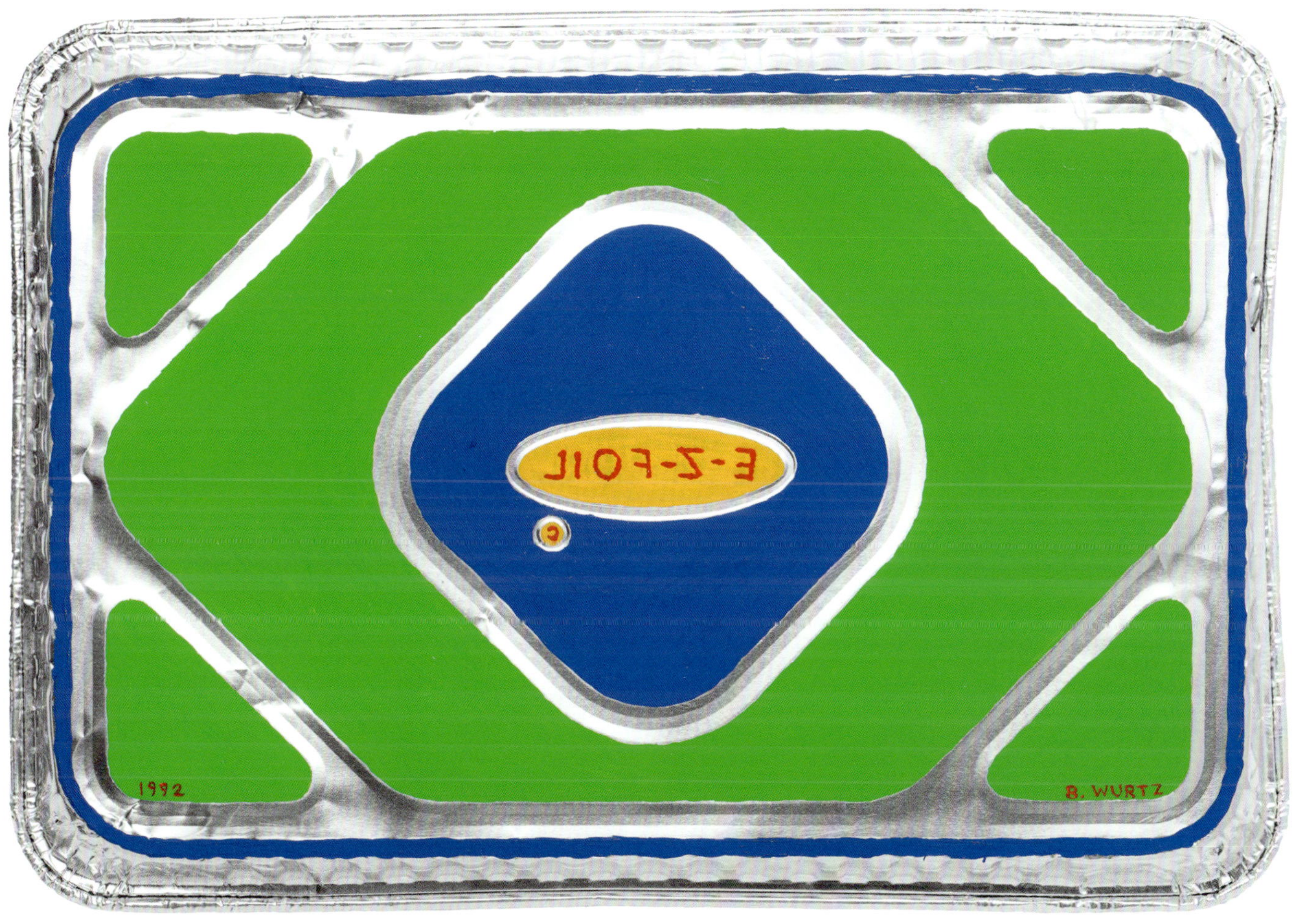

E-Z-FOIL
1992
B. WURTZ

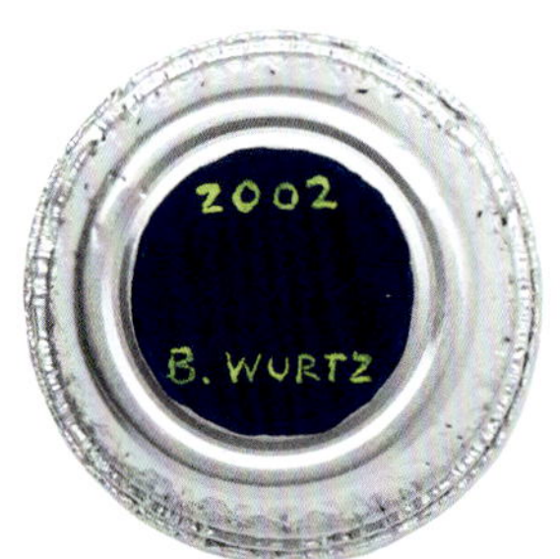
2002
B. WURTZ

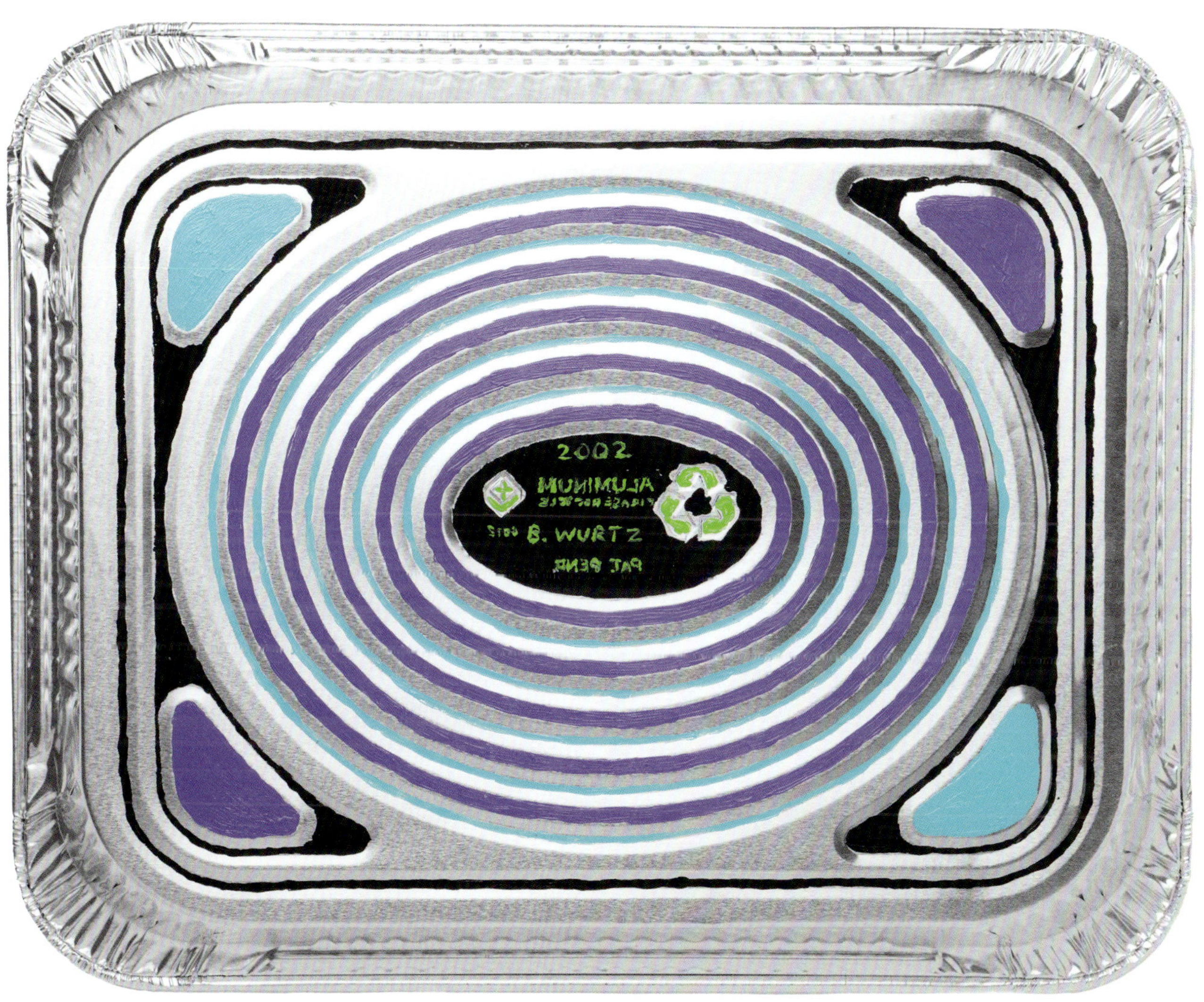

2002
ALUMINUM
B. WURTZ
PAT PEND

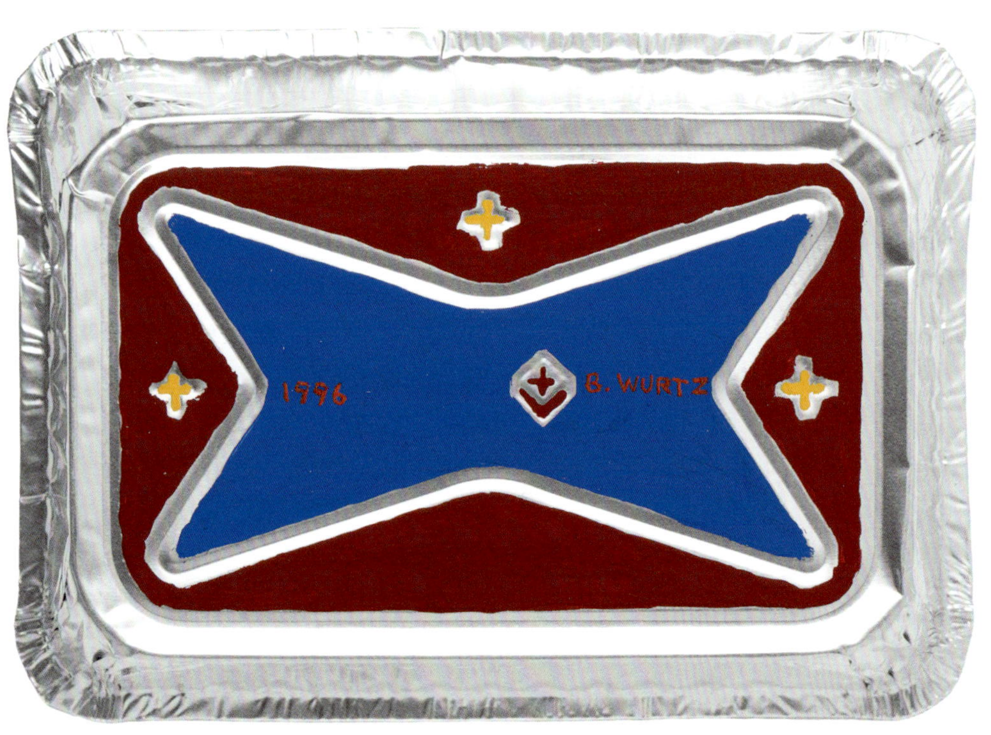

1996
G. WURTZ

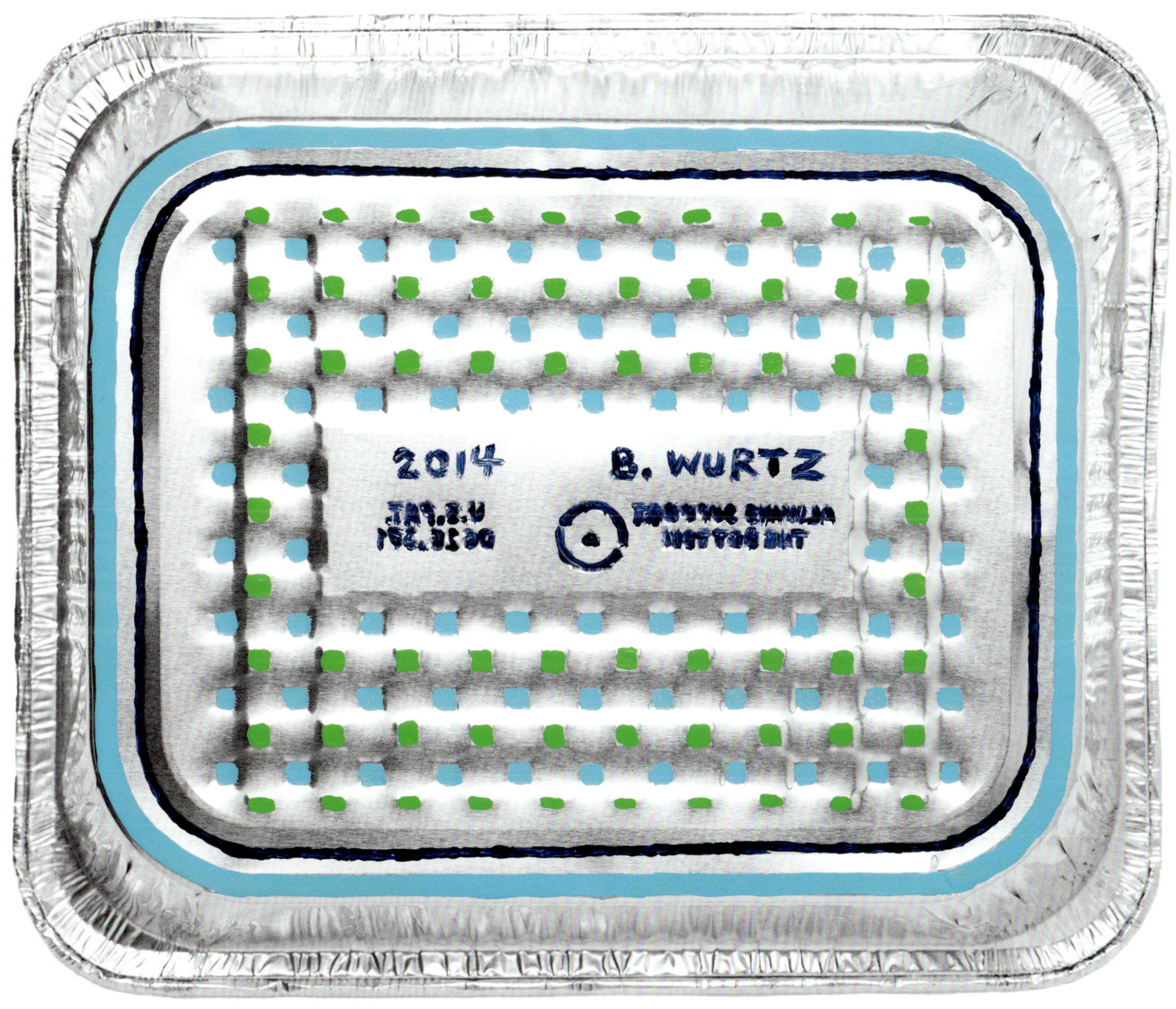

2014
B. WURTZ

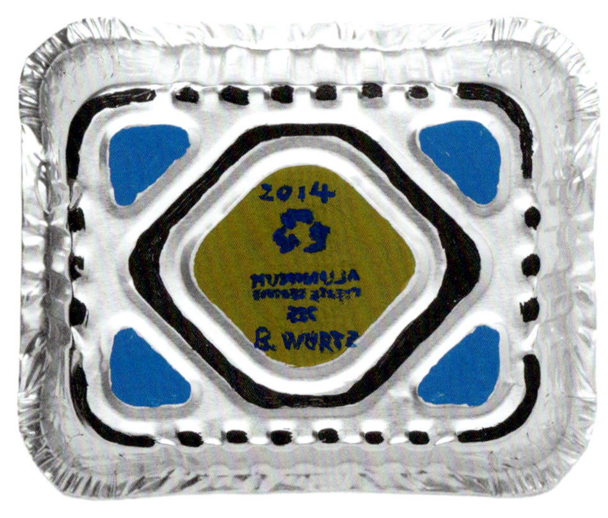

2014
ALUMINUM
Light Gauge
B. WURTZ

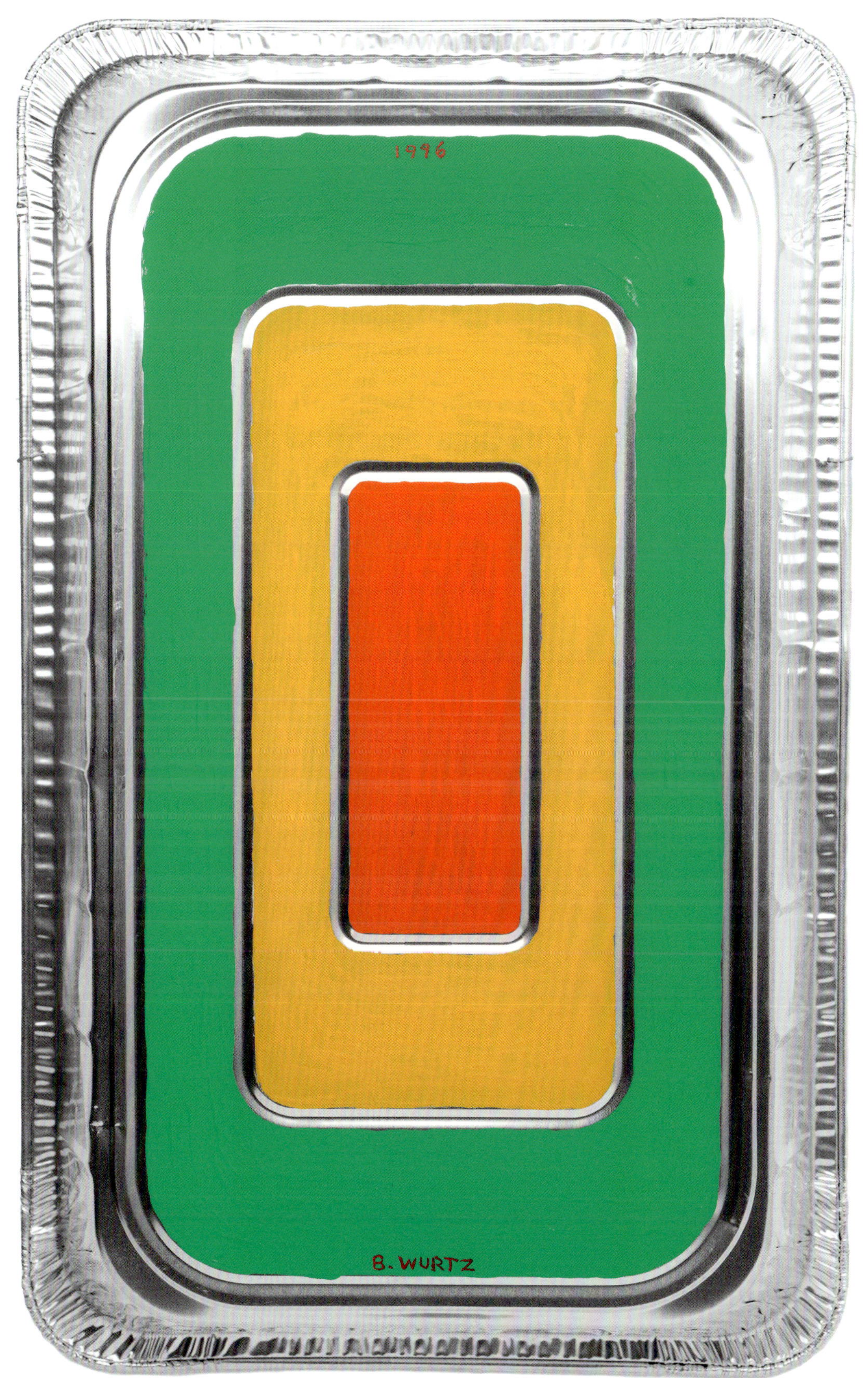

1996
B. WURTZ

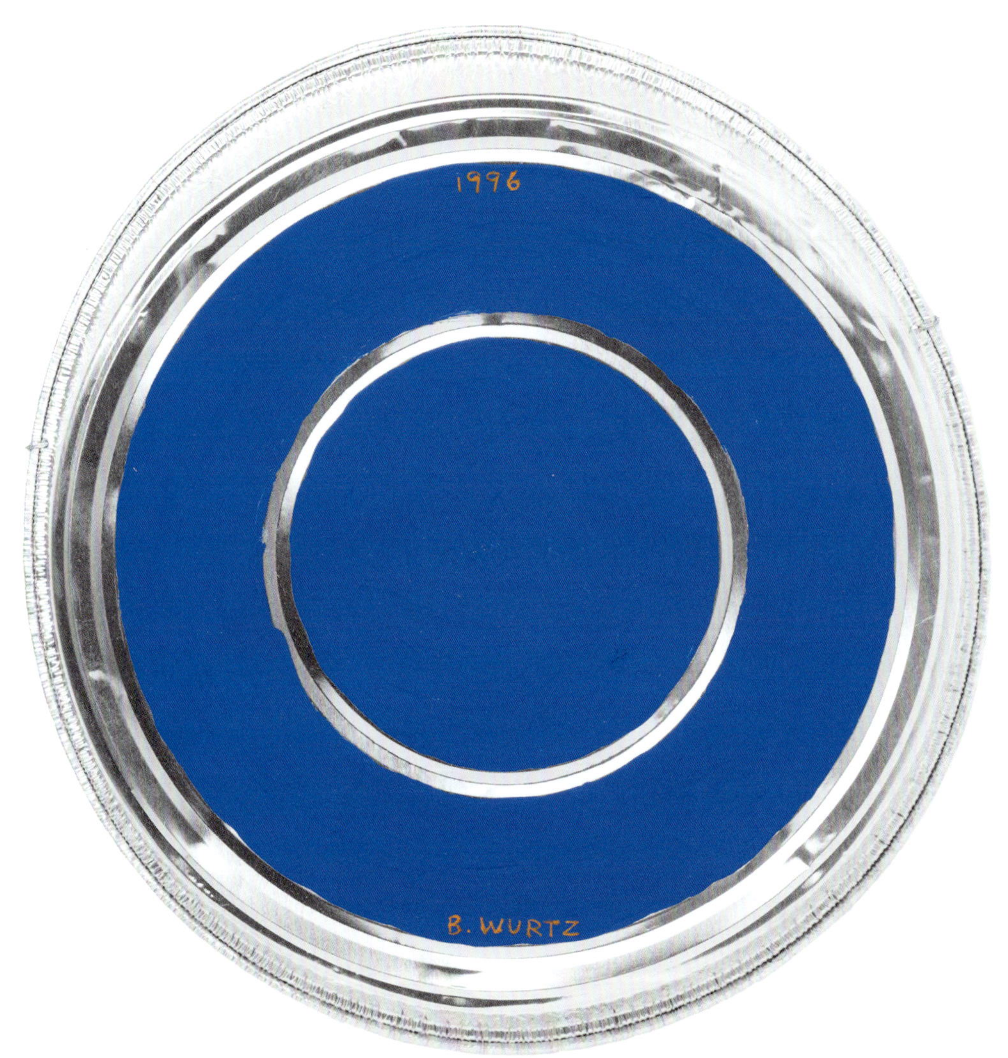

1996
B. WURTZ

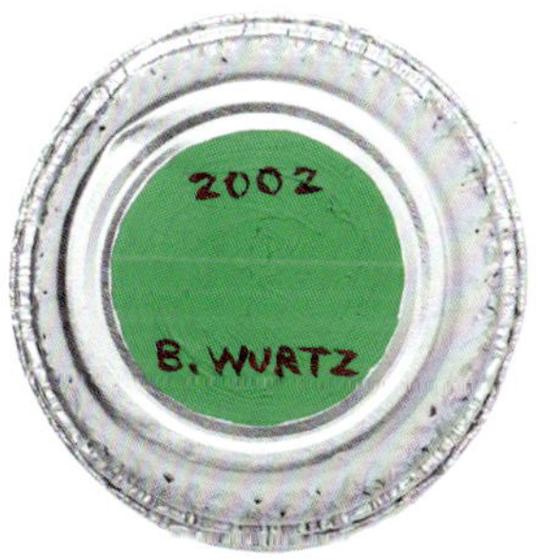
2002
B. WURTZ

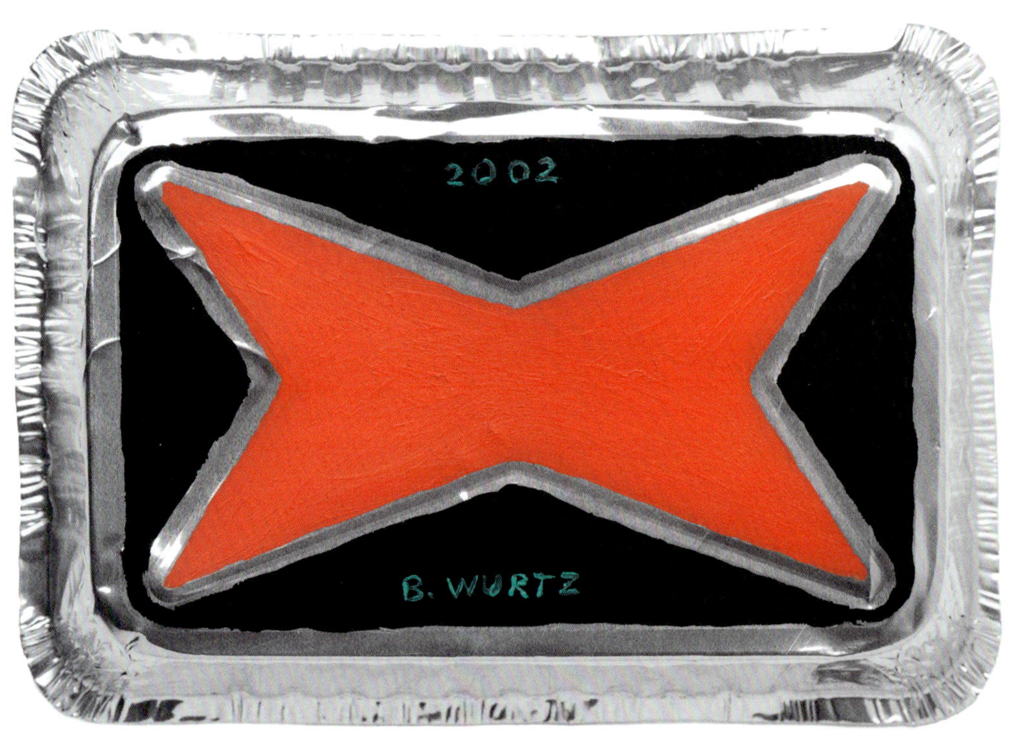
2002
B. WURTZ

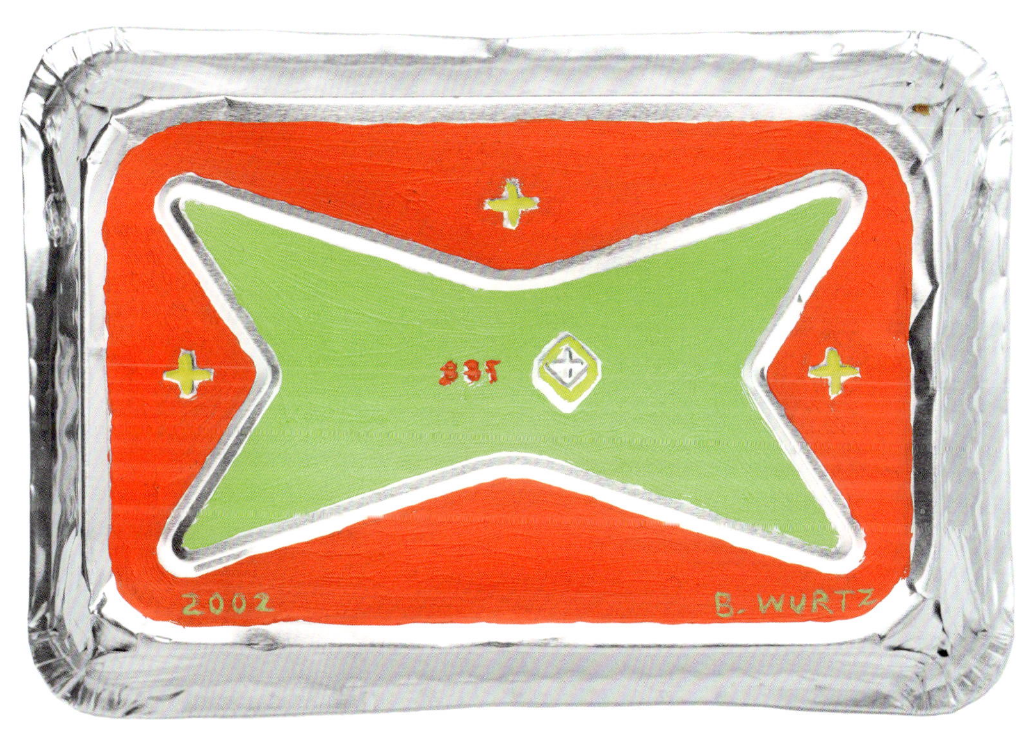

2002
B. WURTZ

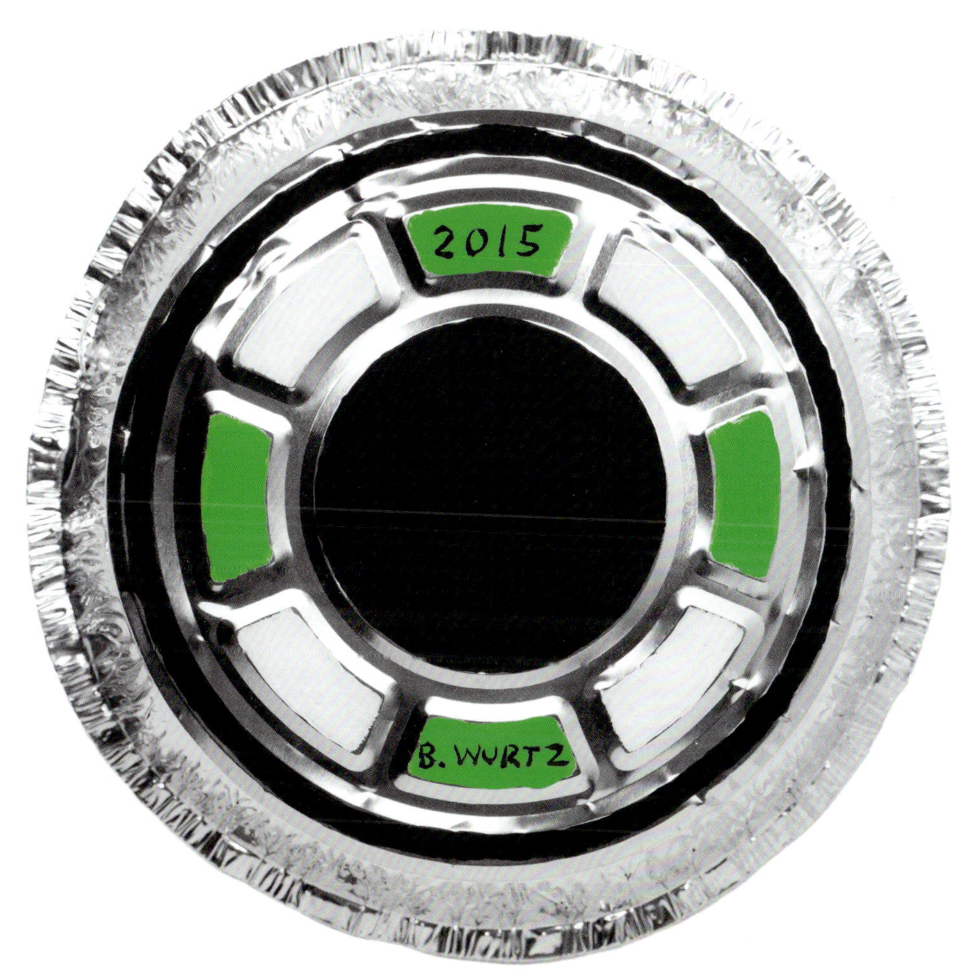
2015
B. WURTZ

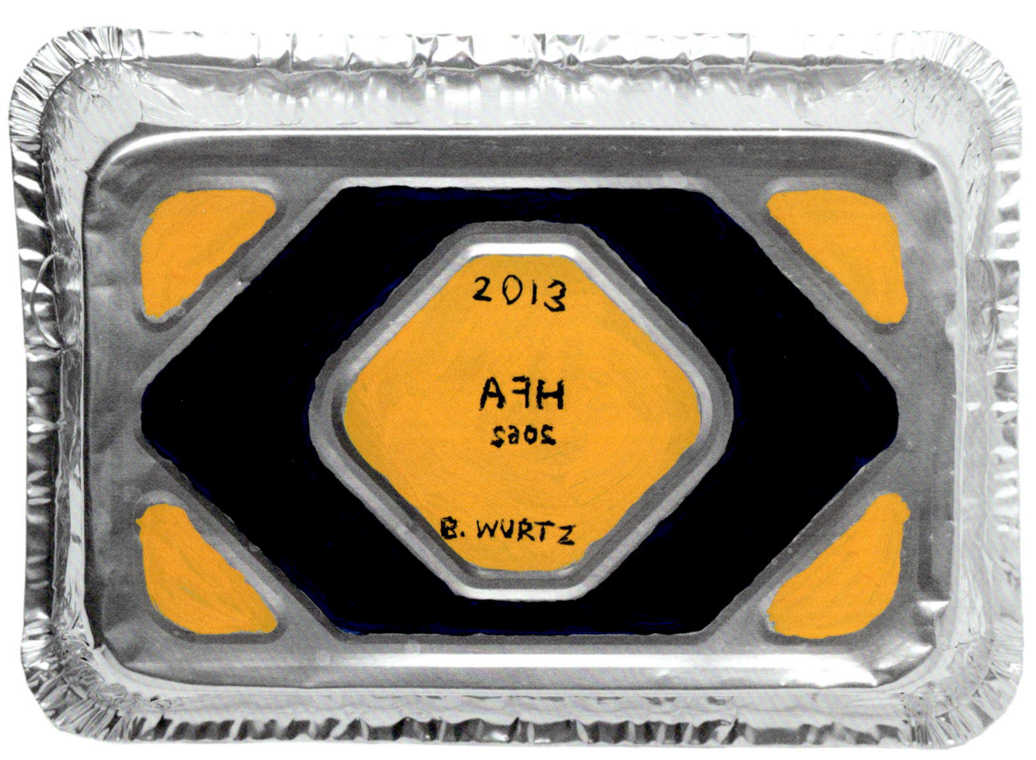

2013
HFA
2013
B. WURTZ

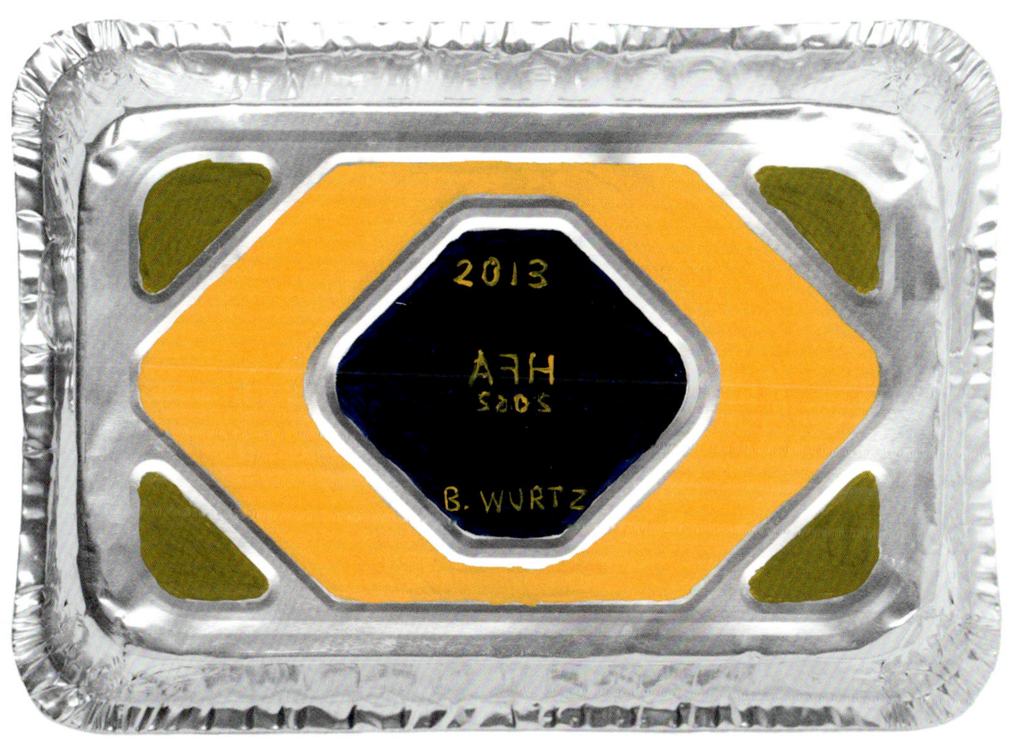

2013
AFH
5005
B. WURTZ

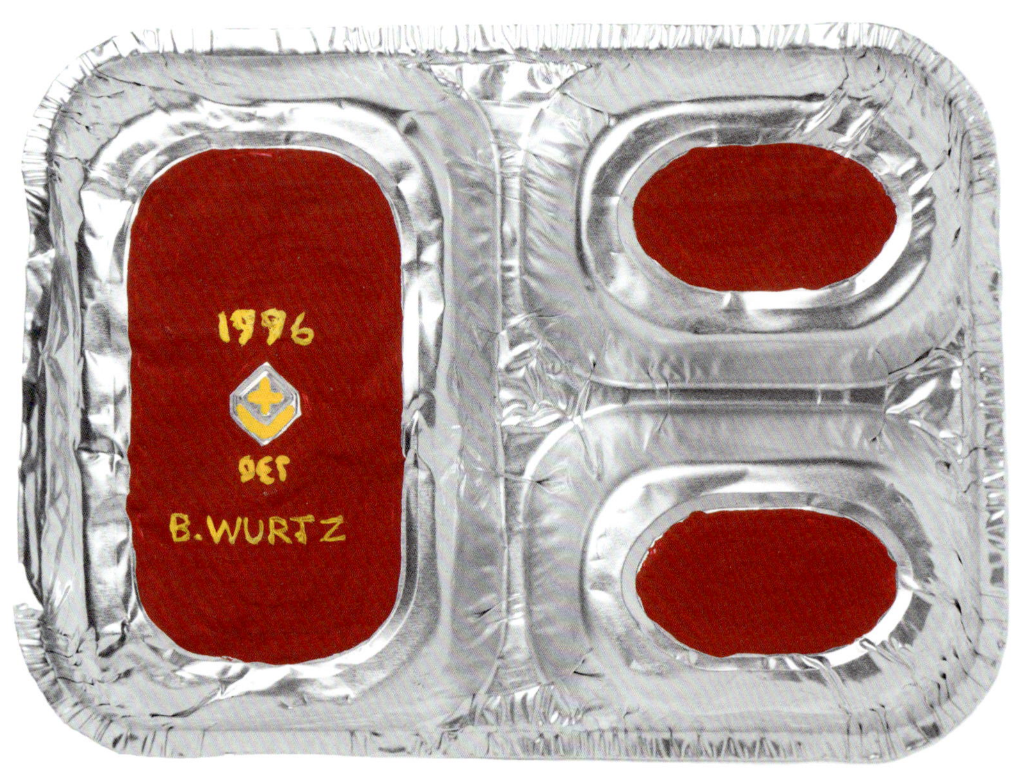

1996
B.WURTZ

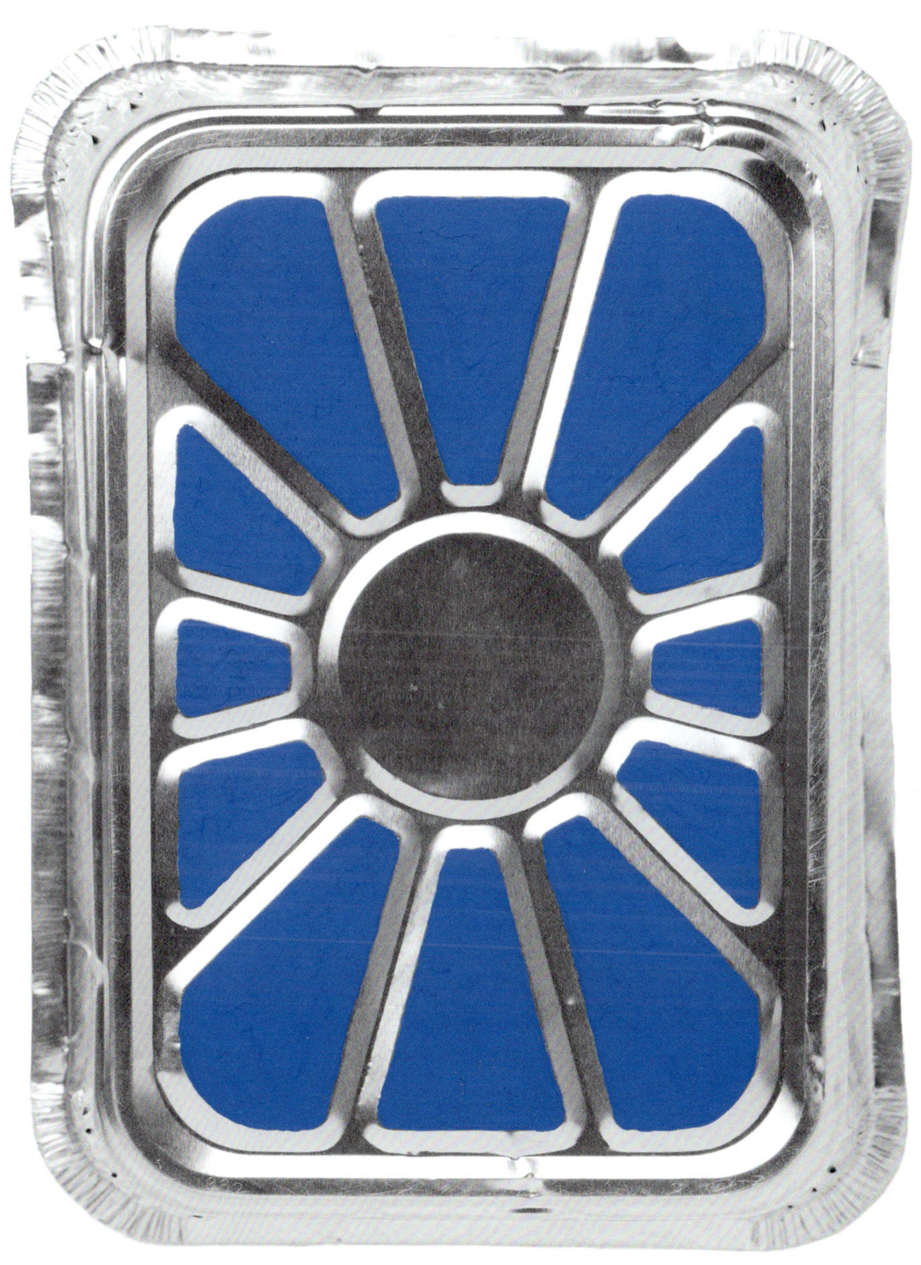

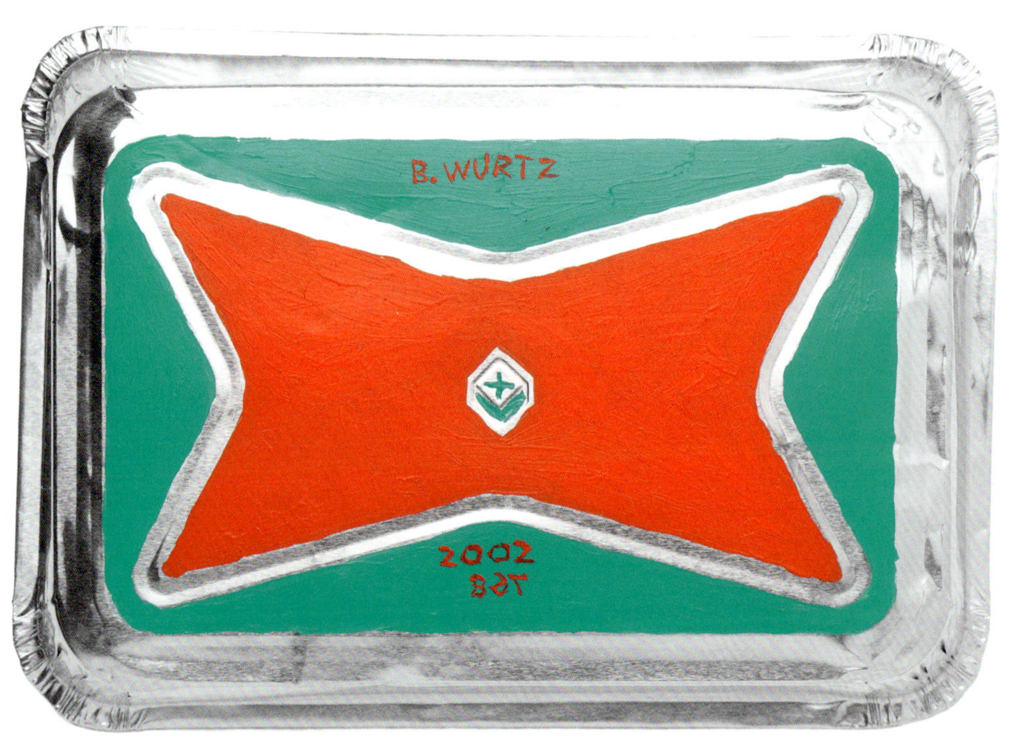

B. WURTZ
2002
768

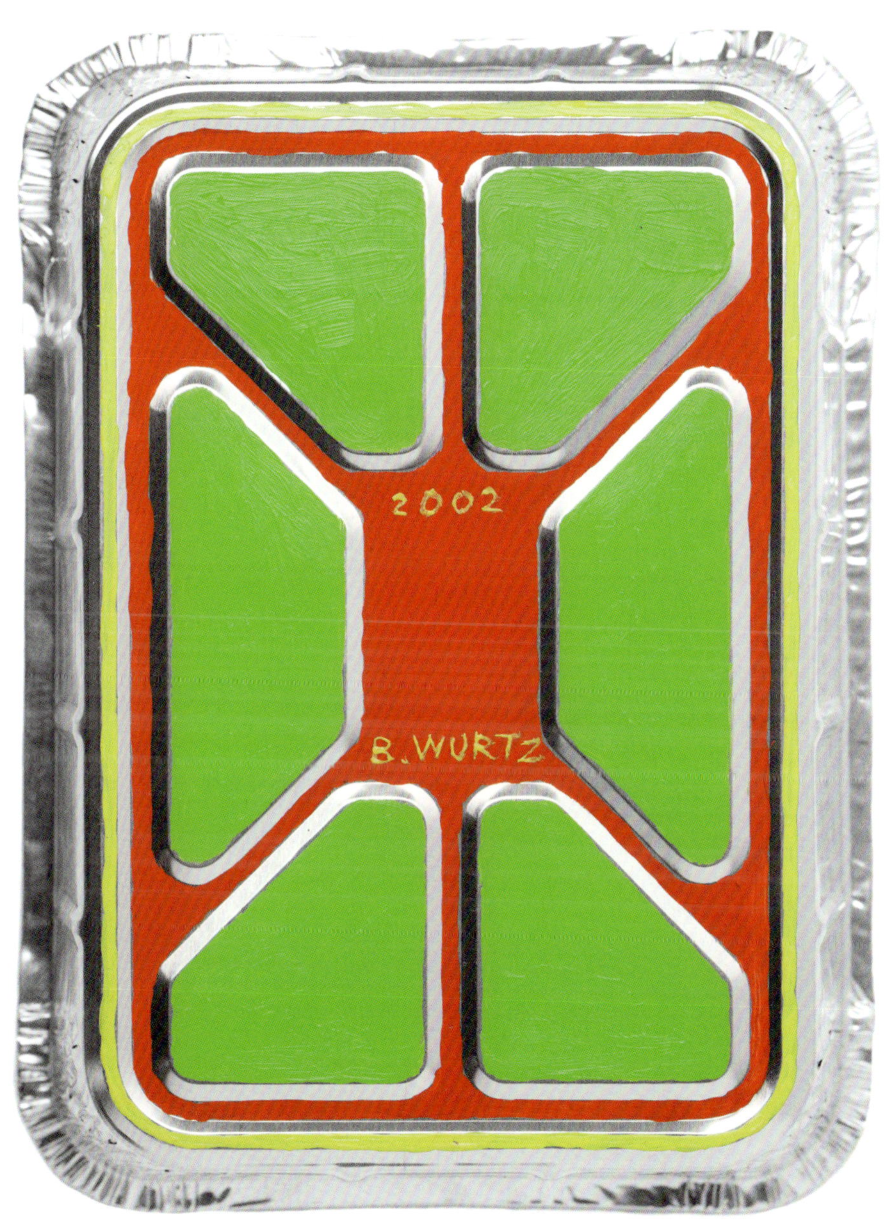

2002
B.WURTZ

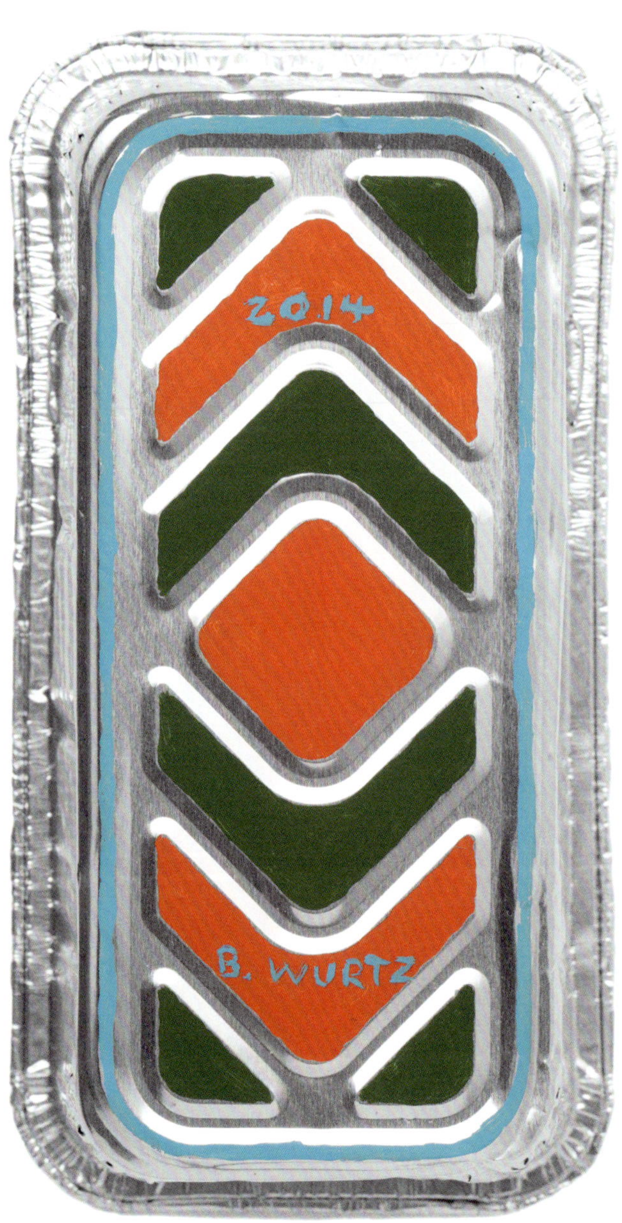

2014
B. WURTZ

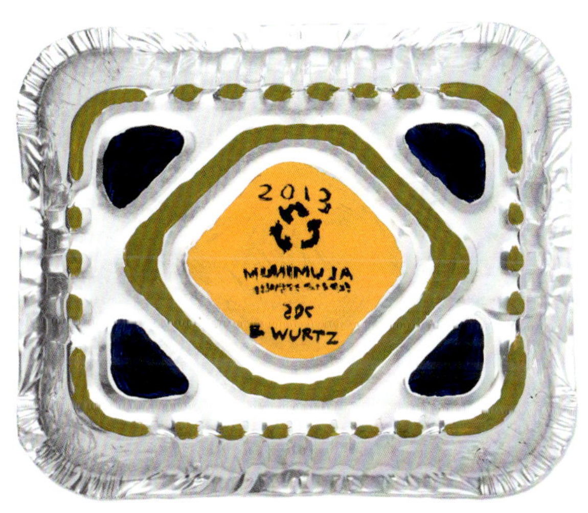
2013
ALUMINUM
B WURTZ

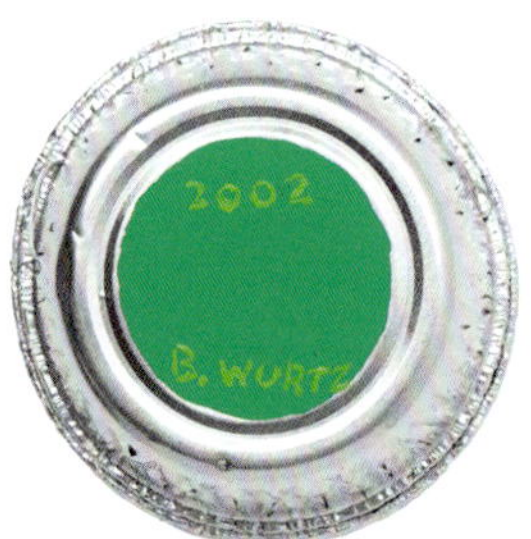
2002
B. WURTZ

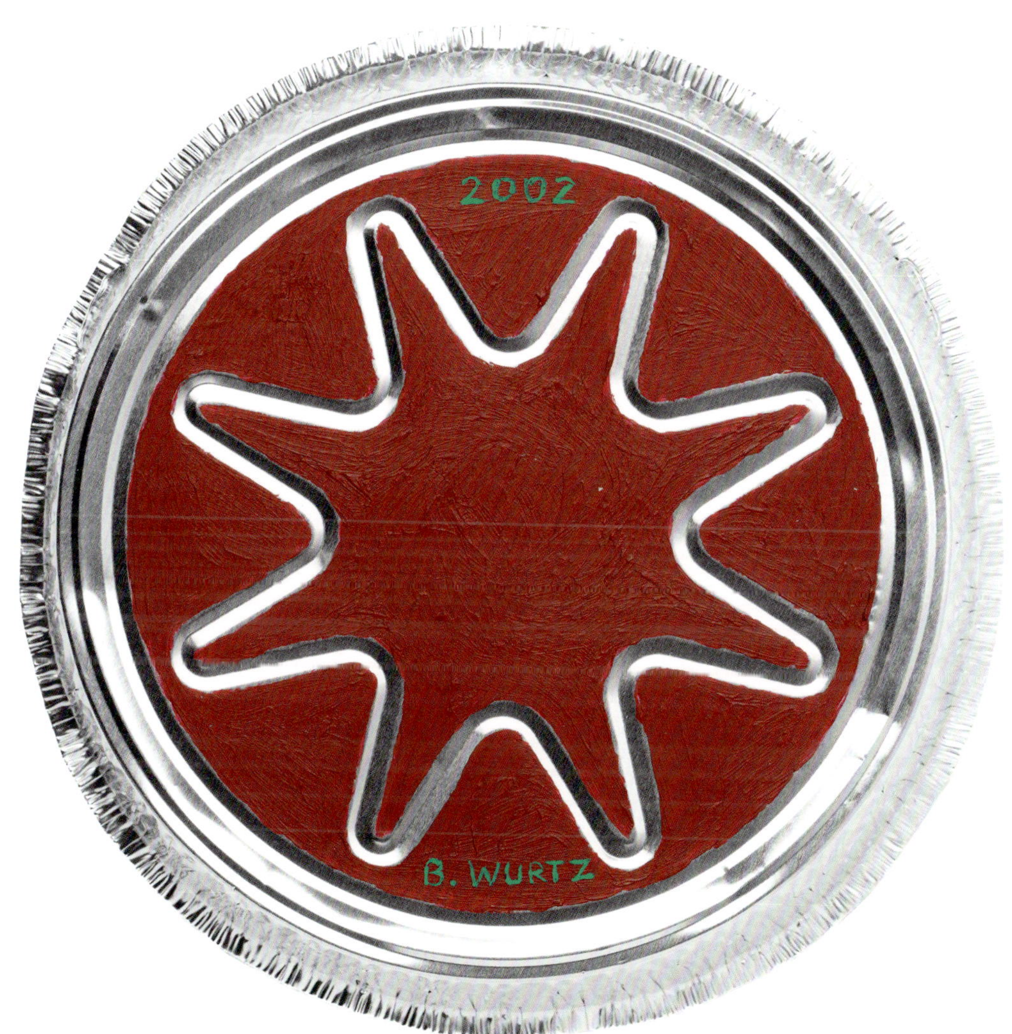

2002
B. WURTZ

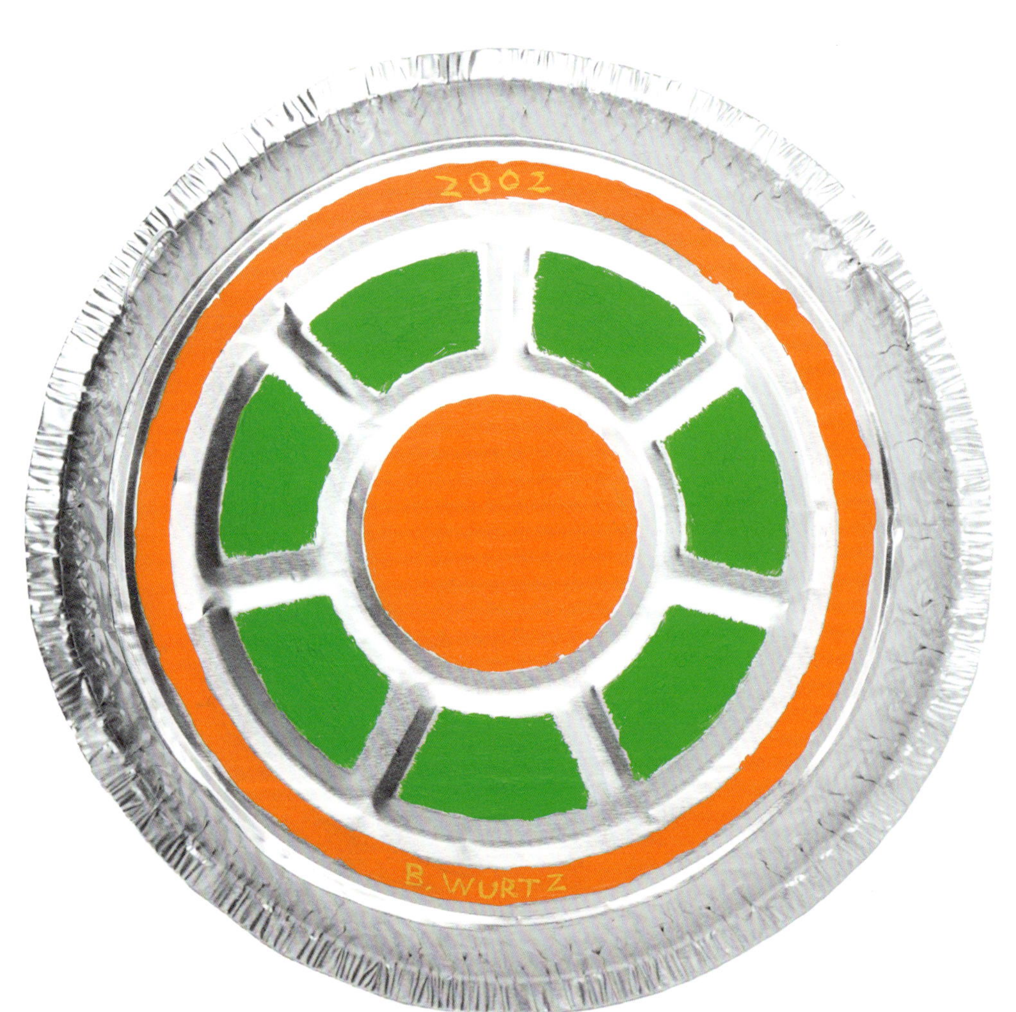

2002
B. WURTZ

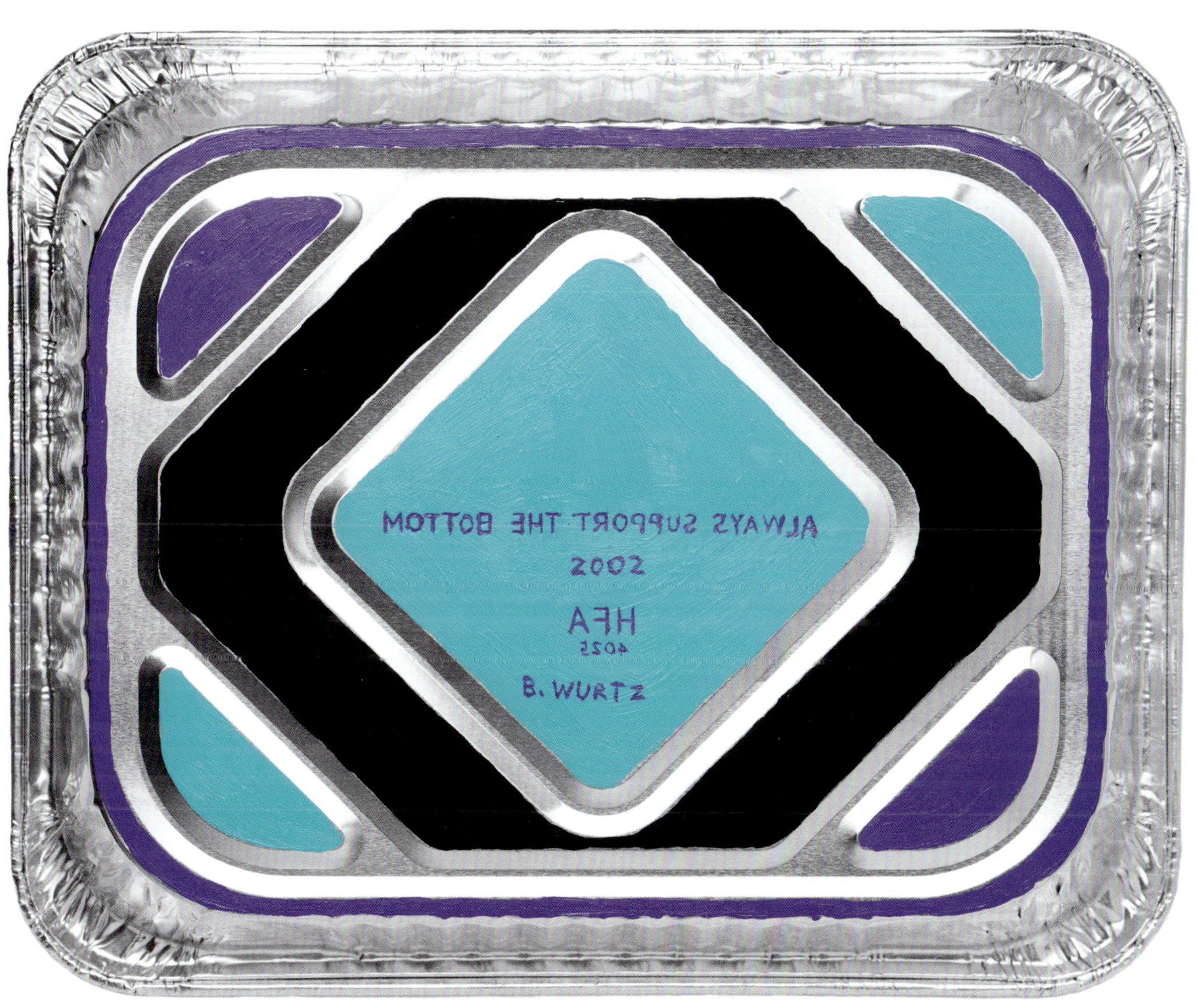

ALWAYS SUPPORT THE BOTTOM
2002
HFA
2504
B. WURTZ

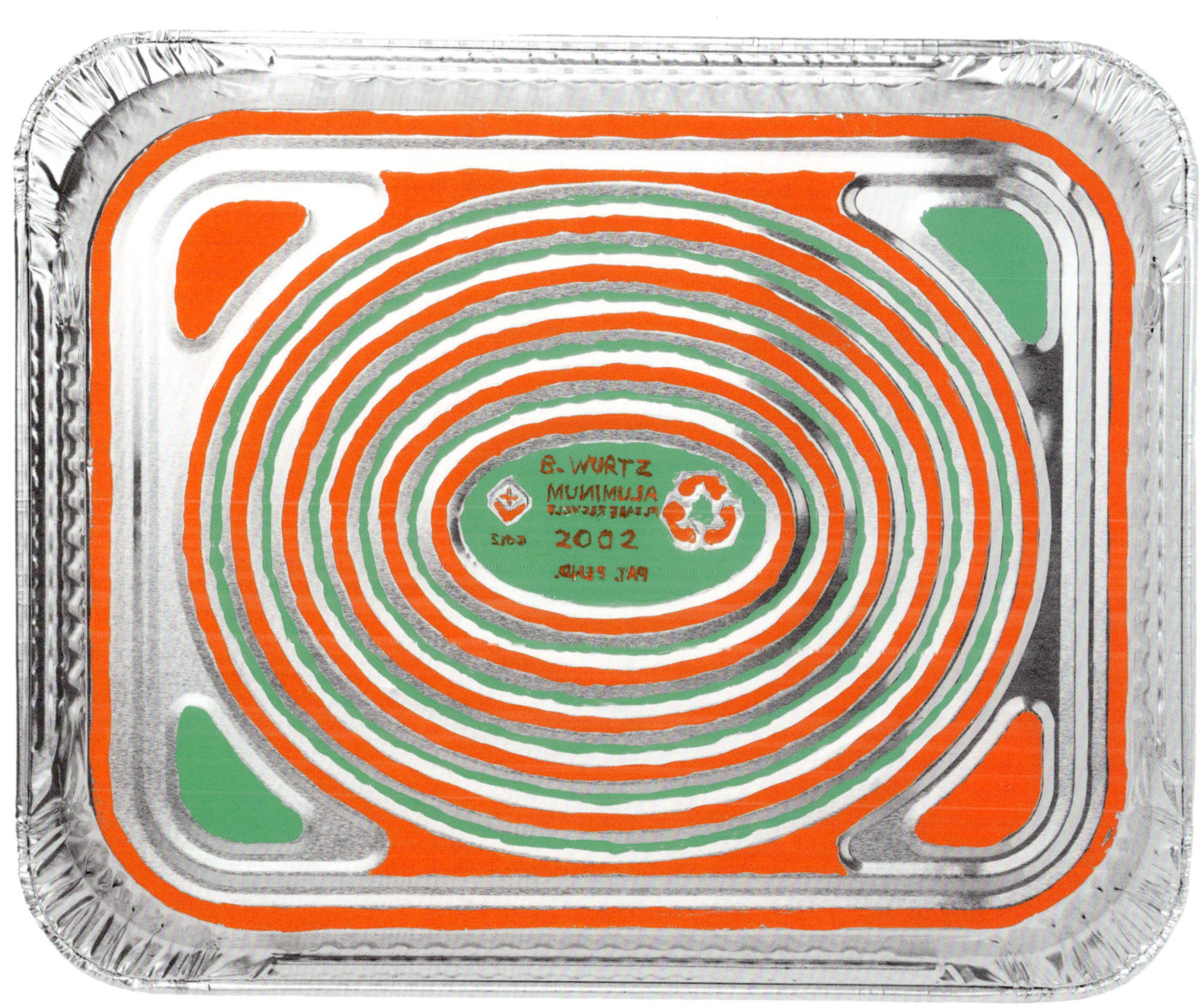
B. WURTZ
ALUMINUM
PLEASE RECYCLE
2002
PAT. PEND.

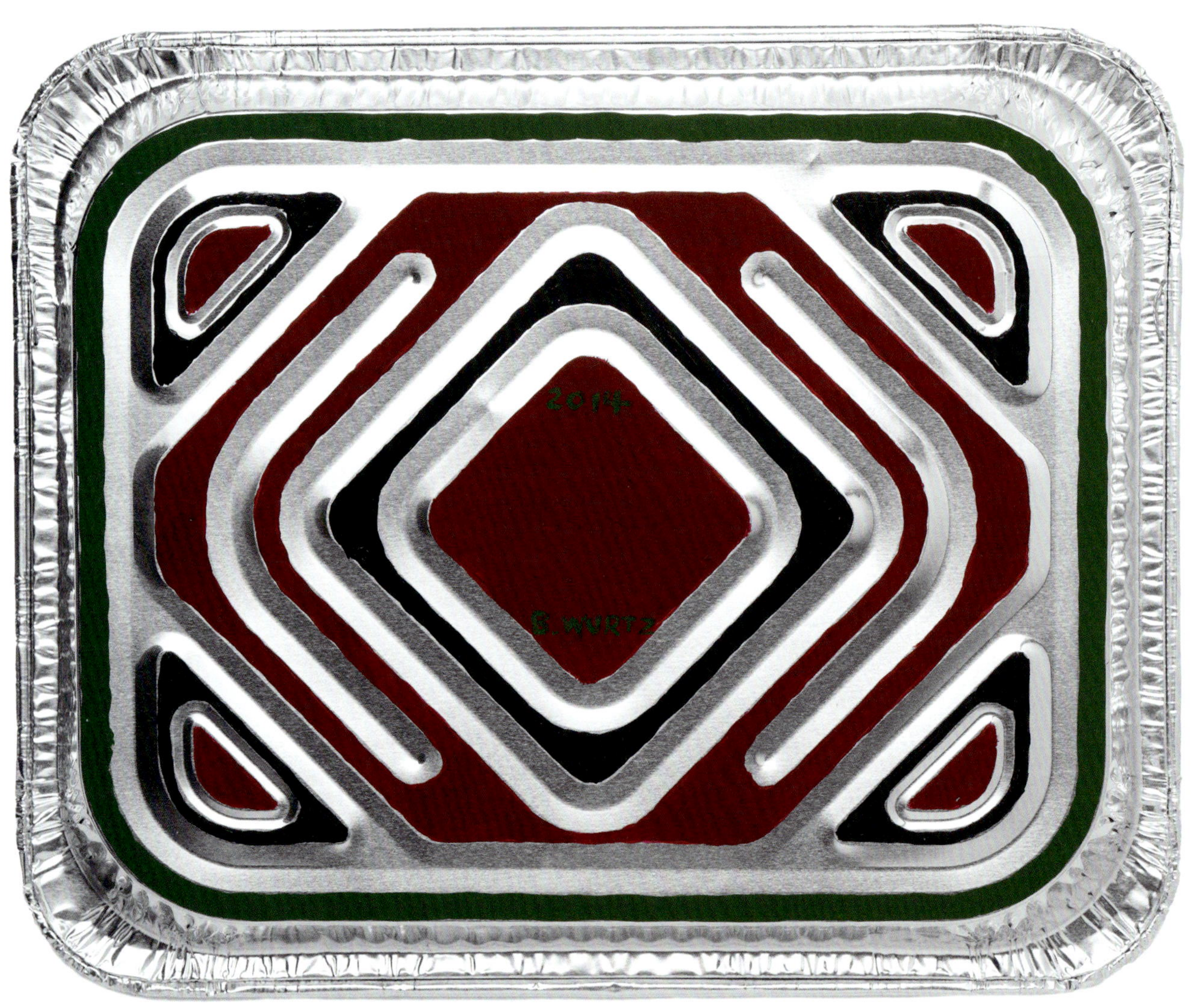

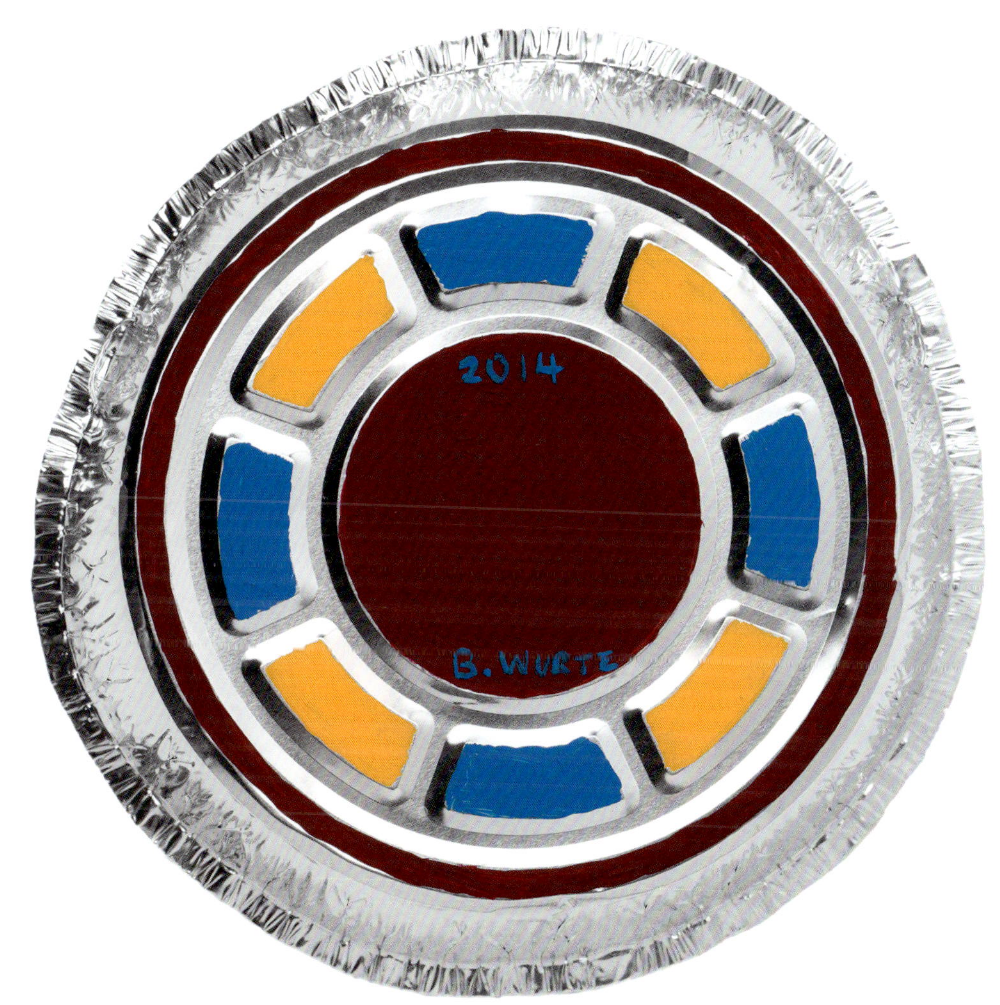

2014
B. WURTE

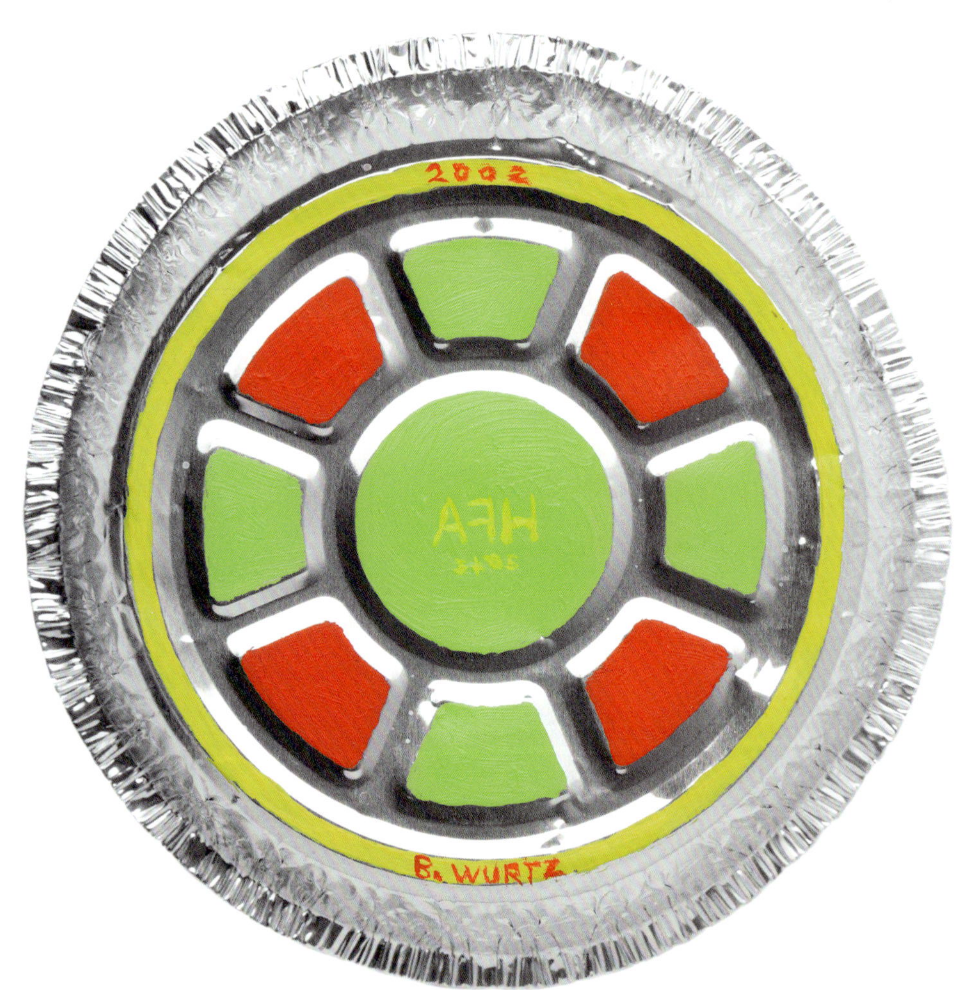
2002
B. WURTZ

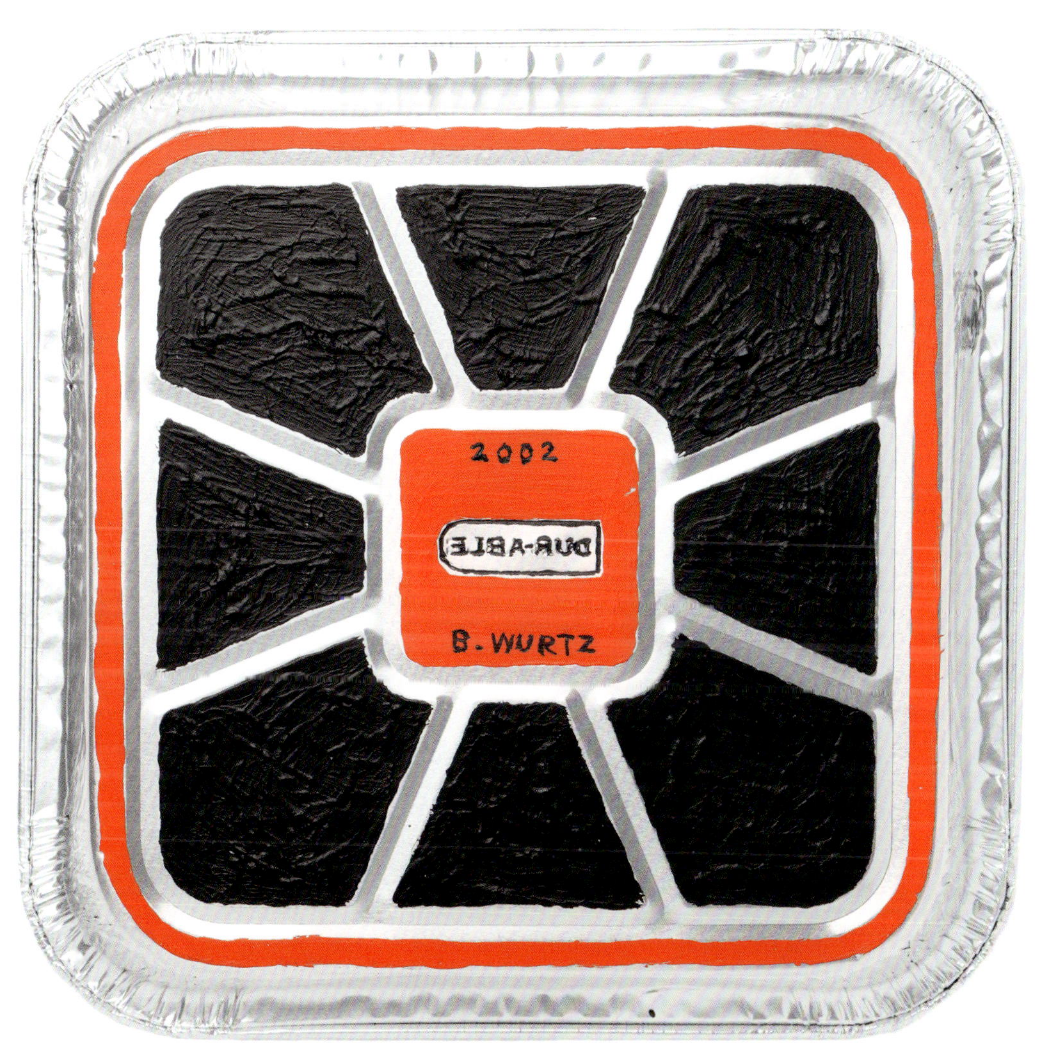
2002
DUR-ABLE
B. WURTZ

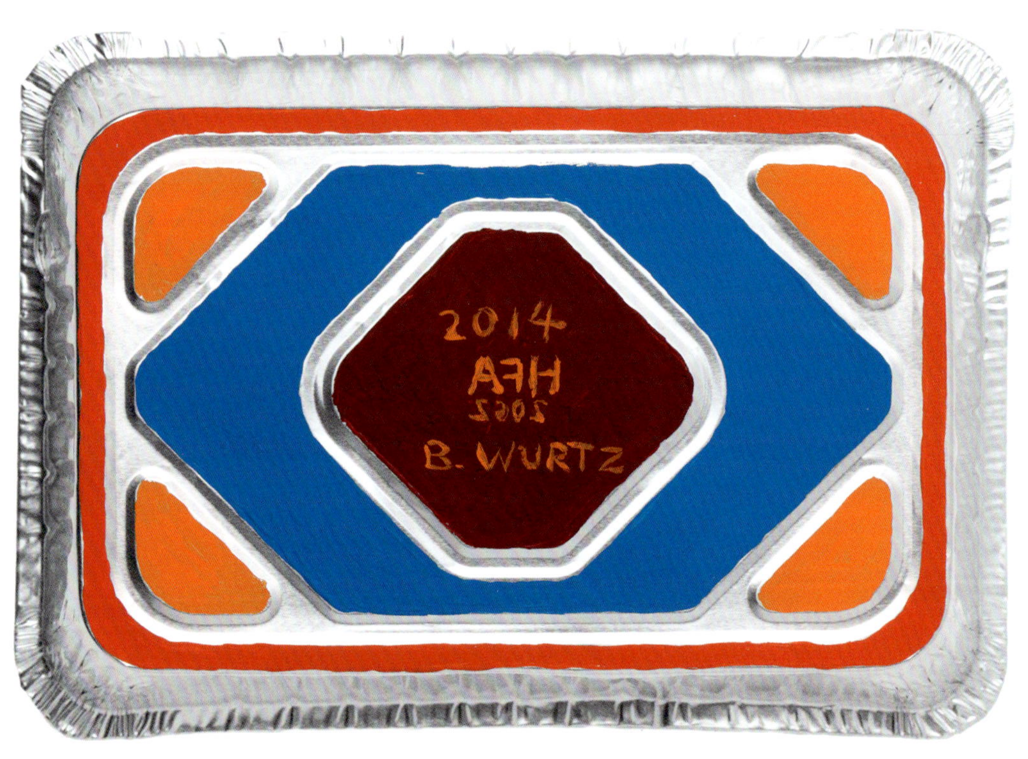

2014
AFA
B. WURTZ

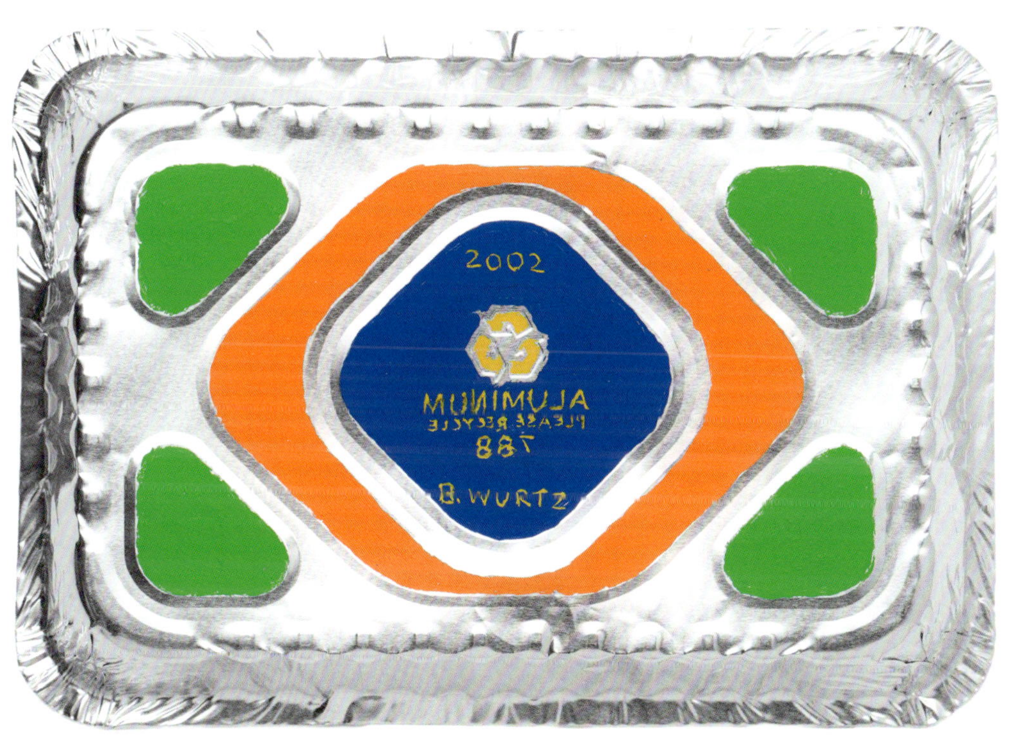

2002
ALUMINUM
PLEASE RECYCLE
788
B. WURTZ

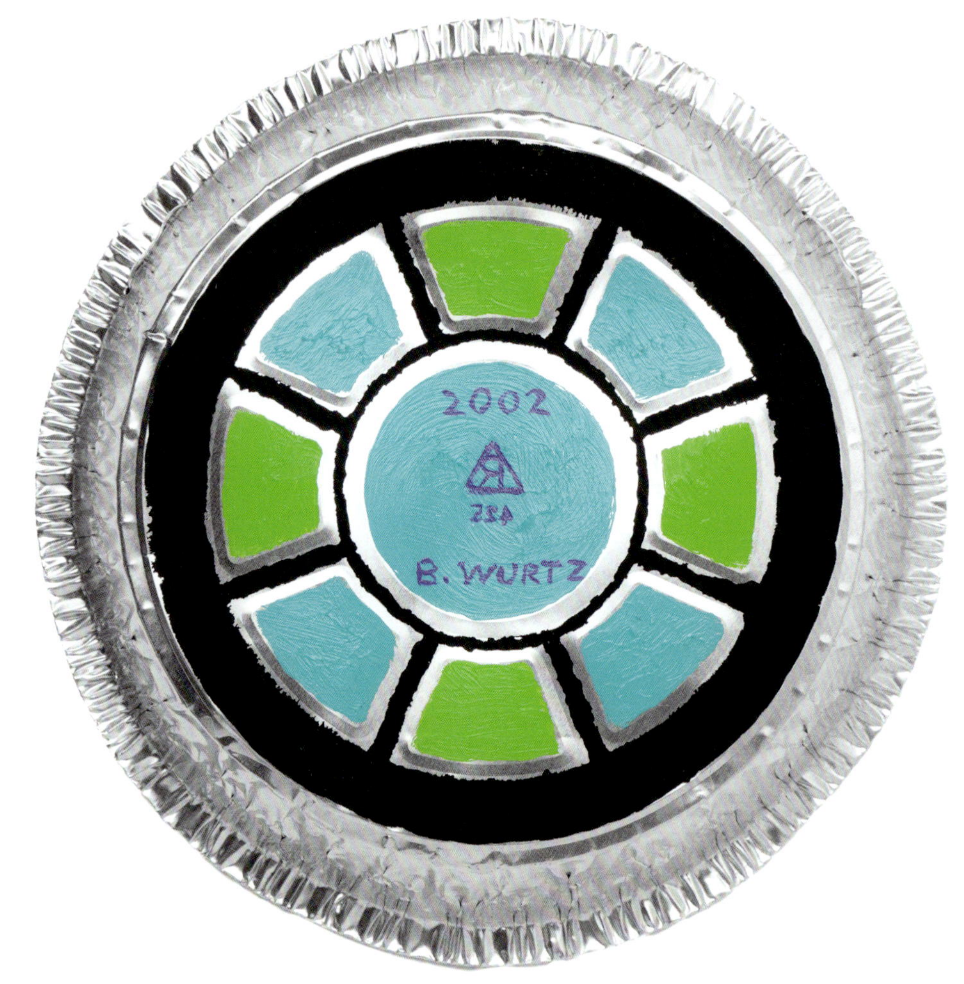
2002
B. WURTZ

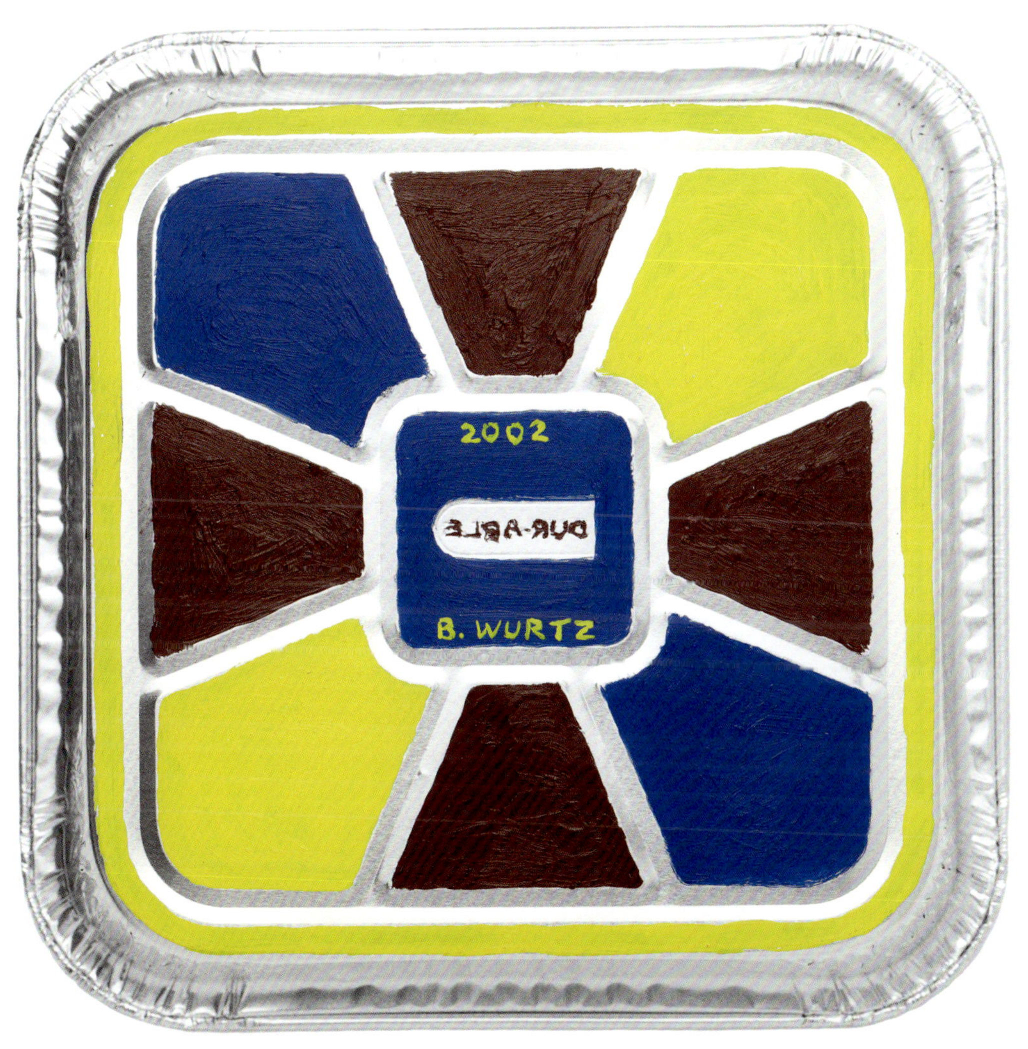

2002
DUR-ABLE
B. WURTZ

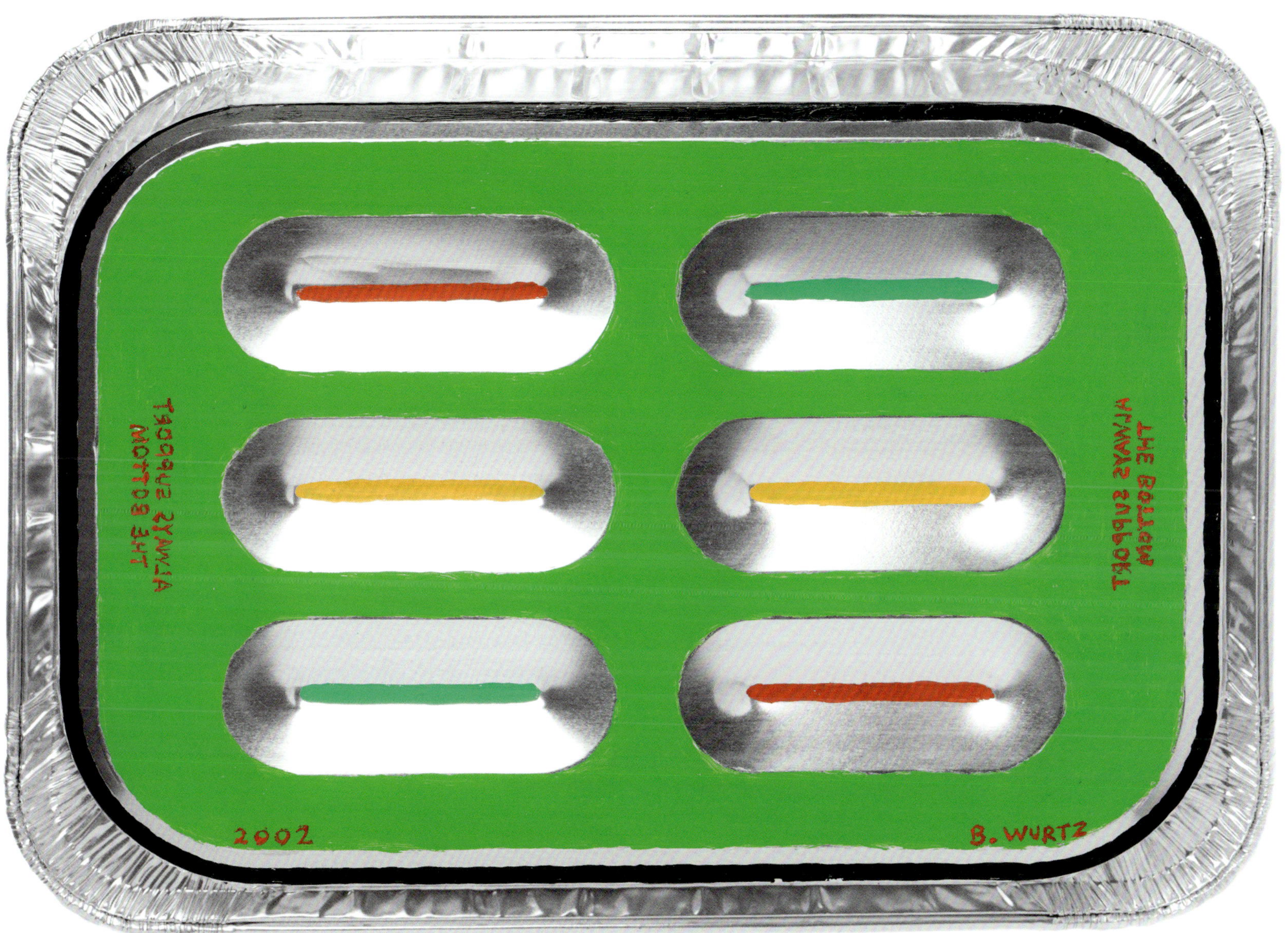

2002
B. WURTZ

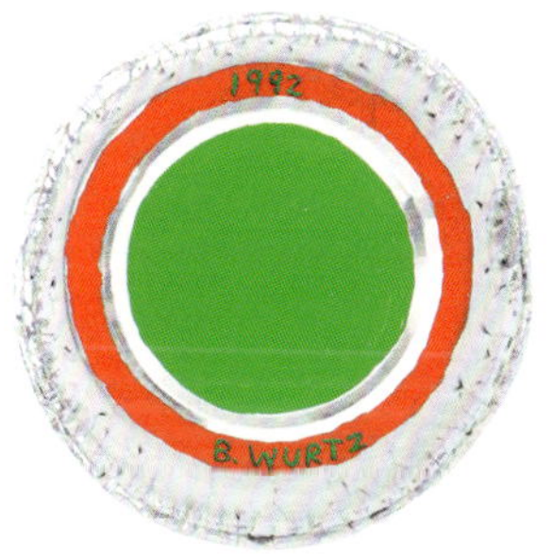
1992
B. WURTZ

OVEN-READY-MADE

Erica Cooke

When artist B. Wurtz accounts for the genesis of his *Pan Paintings*, an ongoing series in which he applies various hues of acrylic paint to the bottom of aluminum food pans, he describes how he initially amassed his raw materials: "The first [pan] was a smallish round one that was part of a food delivery to our apartment in New York. There was no mandatory recycling at that time in the city, but I had been saving the aluminum pans and taking them to a community recycling center in the West Village."[1] These disposable items, after transporting food from restaurant to residence (and after occasional reuse for storing leftovers), become used material to be discarded. Wurtz, however, interrupted the destiny of these waste products: after noticing the stamped patterns on the bottoms of these pans—and grasping their potential as ready-made abstractions—he decided to collect these mass-produced wares and transform them by applying paint.

"All I had to do was add the color," he notes, granting partial authorship to the anonymous industrial designers who determined the surface motifs that, in turn, give shape to Wurtz's fields of flat, unmodulated color.[2] At the moment the artist encounters an intriguing aluminum pan, it already exists as a half-baked painting to be completed with color.

Wurtz limits the materials he employs for his art practice to those related to food, clothing, and shelter—three categories that he deems fundamental for survival and happiness.[3] The artist thus envisions disposable aluminum pans with an optimist's eye: instead of representing the undesired remains of the past, he views them as imbued with potential for the future. Wurtz's *Pan Paintings*—the first was made in 1990, and the series is ongoing, with over five hundred examples at the time of this writing—call attention to the nature of amateur culture in America through their repurposing of

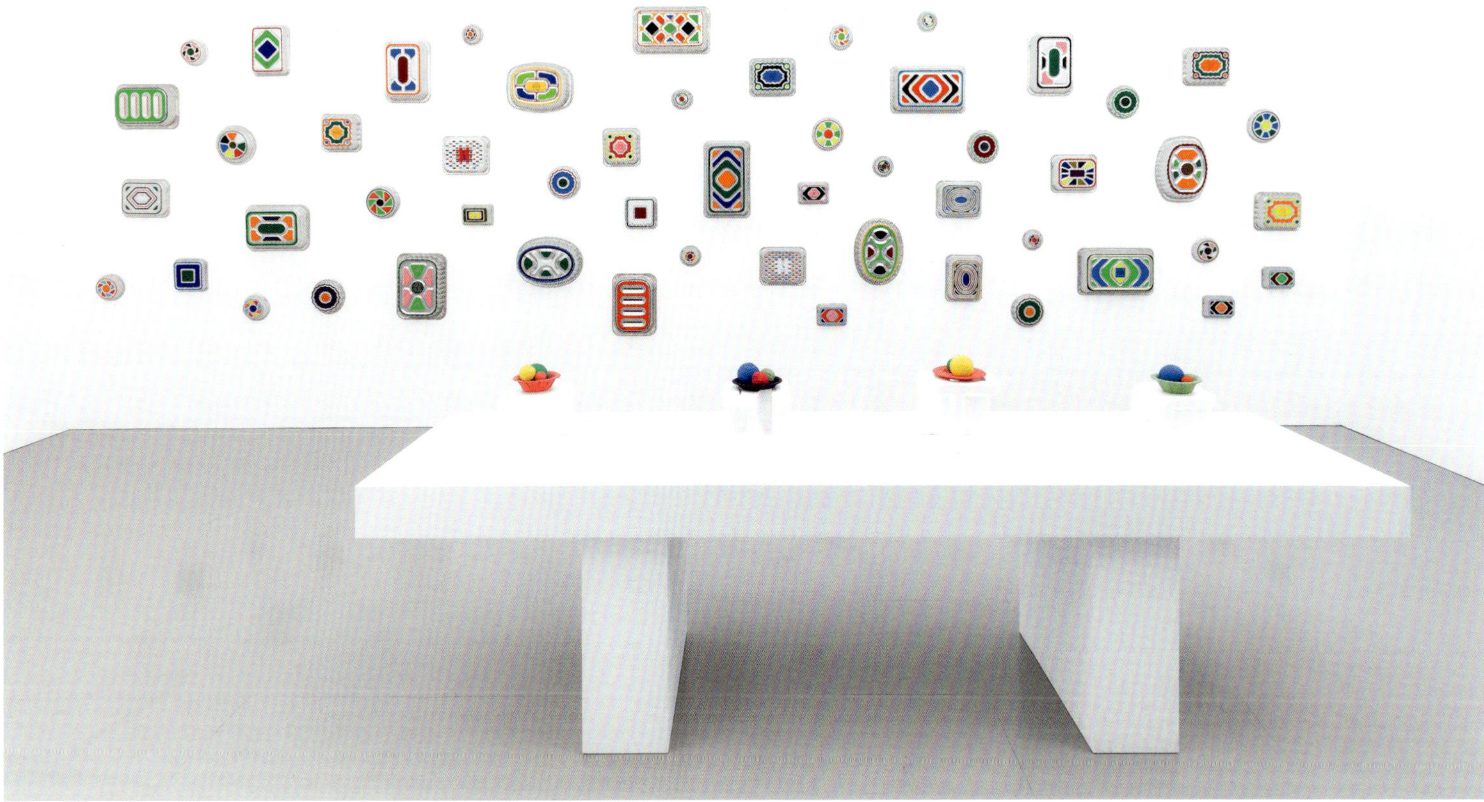

these everyday materials. Much ink has been spilled over how to define "amateur" art: is it analogous to folk art or outsider art, indicating that the practice lies beyond mainstream and institutional parameters? Does the artist's general knowledge, academic training, or cultural exposure establish the designation? The boundaries of amateurism in art have become increasingly contested as contemporary artists (those typically deemed "professional") have taken up certain characteristics associated with it, particularly the use of a studied naïveté with respect to technical skill. The aim may be to blur categorical distinctions, but the effect only reinforces the stereotype that amateurs exist in binary and unequal opposition to professionals: that is, the "amateur" has not yet attained—and perhaps could never attain—professional status.

To treat amateurism as a leasable concept, a sort of role-playing exercise for professionals, fails to acknowledge the term's specific history in America. The amateur artist was not historically defined in opposition to the professional one (i.e., the artist who progressed through formalized art studies and thence into galleries and public collections), as amateurism predates the emergence in the 1950s of contemporary art-world professionalism in the United States. It began to pervade American culture as early as the 1930s with the establishment of the Works Progress Administration (1935–43). The WPA's nationwide mandate to provide federal employment and funding for thousands of artists lent credence to the belief that the making of art and crafts was a central part of the American experience, one worthy of special appreciation. Fostering aspirations for artists and audiences alike foregrounded the populist interest in everyday life and objects: the director of the WPA's Federal Art Project, Holger Cahill, spearheaded an initiative

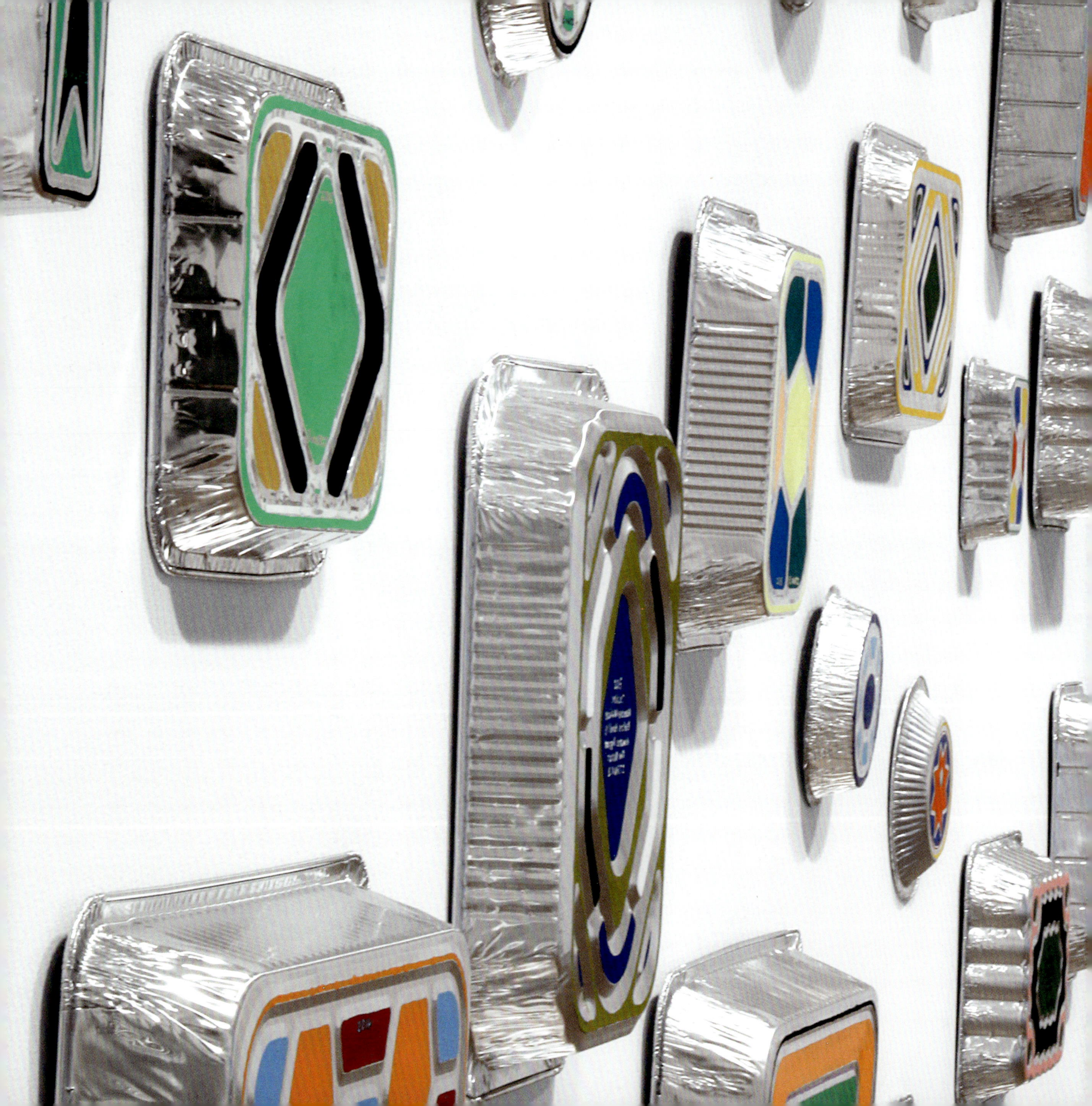

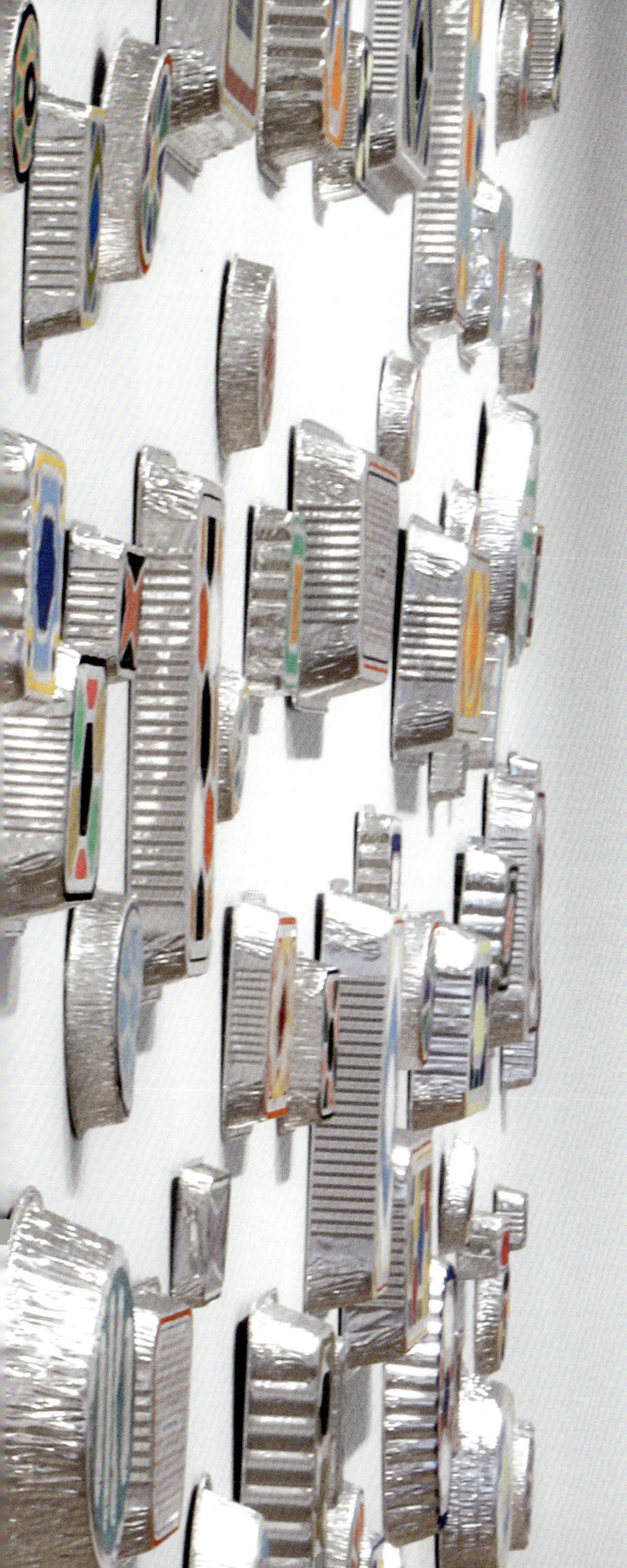

known as the Index of American Design, a project that employed skilled illustrators and graphic designers to document over eighteen thousand examples of American decorative art objects in highly realistic watercolors.

The purpose of the Index was to preserve the country's expansive traditions of object-making, which underscored local character and material proficiency. Artistic training mattered, but not in the sense of "professional" credentials; rather, emphasis was placed on familiarity with regional traditions and the requisite acquisition of needed skills, whether by formal or informal means.[4] In effect, the etymology of *amateur*—derived from the Latin for to love—befits the New Deal era's pedagogical directive to cultivate passion for native forms of art, sowing the seeds for a radical field of practice among artists principally concerned with everyday life.[5] Such practices, however, were largely sidelined in the immediate aftermath of World War II and the subsequent decade of the 1950s, when a modernist discourse became ascendant. According to art historian Howard Singerman, the "formalization of art training and the prospect of professionalism in the university" came to pass due to the cohort of soldiers who came back from the war to study on the GI Bill, some of whom populated New York's art schools. This influx, "combined with the critical visibility of an emergent abstract expressionism," in turn integrated the university "with an enlarged professional art world in New York."[6] Thus, the birth of professionalism in the art world was intimately tied to the rise of AbEx and the concurrent belief that alignment with this movement—the first perceived example of a wholly American modern art— was the most expedient path toward achieving recognition and success as a serious artist. By compelling artists to stick to the issues at stake within modernity, this dominant professional model superseded interest in other extant traditions in American art—but only momentarily.

The period of the 1960s, much like the 1930s, ushered in profound social change that spurned establishment values and brought to the fore a class of objects tethered to the wide arena of an artist's lived experience and aligned with the nuanced traditions of the amateur. In 1964, artist Allan Kaprow wrote, "I suspect that [artists' identities] will have more to do with the aisles in supermarkets than with the aisles in houses of God; more with U.S. Highway 1 in a Ford Mustang than the True Path; more with social psychology than Judeo-Christianity."[7] Moreover, Kaprow advised, "It is right to attach a pair of pants to a canvas. It is true to life to compose a work that perishes with the occasion,"[8] threading postwar art in America through the needle of middle-class society and its do-it-yourself ethos. Shifting from the conventional expectation that art should transcend, extract from, or even elevate the everyday, Kaprow advocated for artists' embeddedness within the everyday through the use of common objects and freedom from the ideology of visual instruction or the exalted language of sublimity associated with AbEx—e.g., of a higher being dictating how and where to pin that "pair of pants."

■ ▢ ▢

Indications of Wurtz's commitment to the prosaic aspects of daily existence—his amateurism, so to speak—are ubiquitous, if not foundational to understanding his work. Wurtz maintains an inventory of items for potential use in his artwork that do not fit the conventional description of collectibles: wire clothes hangers, single-use plastic bags, yogurt lids, shoelaces, and, of course, aluminum pans. These household items have a marked relationship to the human body: they are held, manipulated, eaten out of. The artist's career-long fascination with such quotidian yet pervasive items underscores his embodiment of the amateur archetype as a lover of things—perhaps most evident in his thirty-plus years devoted to thinking about disposable pans.

While large-scale manufacturing often precludes the proliferation of various models for a given commercial product, disposable aluminum pans flout this tenet, constituting a category of mass-produced items that considerably exceeds one-size-fits-all. For Wurtz, the combination of three variable factors—the size, shape, and stamped surface pattern of each pan—provides a compelling set of permutations for his long-running series. To describe a few of these consistent configurations for which there are multiple examples: the medium-size circular pan—8.5 inch diameter—impressed with what appears to be a spiked sphere (plates 7, 12, 23, and 55); the large rectangle—20.75 inches by 13 inches—embossed with three nesting squares with rounded edges (plates 28 and 40); the medium square—8.75 inches by 8.75 inches—stamped with an graphic petal-like design (plates 62 and 66); and the small circle—3.25 inch diameter—with no embossed pattern, like a period at the end of a sentence (plates 2, 15, 35, 42, 54, and 68). As these examples make clear, even when Wurtz deploys identical pans, this does not yield uniform results, because he applies various hues to the pans' stamped patterns and occasionally alters the customary orientation for hanging a given pan shape by 90 degrees.

Oftentimes Wurtz highlights indications of the machine-made and utilitarian nature of these pans—for example, he applies specific colors to the embossed letters of product specifications (DUR-ABLE and 100% RECYCLED ALUMINUM) (plates 57, 62, and 5, respectively) as well as instructional text (ALWAYS SUPPORT THE BOTTOM). Despite such overt attention paid to the practical use-value of these items, Wurtz does not embrace the signs of wear and tear typical of leftover food containers; none of the *Pan Paintings*, for example, are noticeably indented or have edges bearing hardened crusts of reheated food. Whether through repairing dents, removing food residues, or intentionally collecting impeccable pans, Wurtz's sensibility for this series does not include untidiness. Even his ideal setting for the installation of his pan paintings echoes the cleanliness and clarity of machine-produced objects: the artist prefers a standard white-cube gallery setup, with blank walls and hardwood or concrete floors with well-calibrated lighting. Wurtz also opts for careful yet intuitive arrangements of his pan paintings, often resulting in salon-style hangs on a single large wall. He has been and continues to be flexible about who oversees the installation of his *Pan Paintings*—whether by the curator, art handler, himself, or another individual involved in the exhibition—as long as the overall grouping of pans is neither entirely arbitrary nor tightly adhering to a set of self-imposed guidelines. In essence, the salon-style hang should encourage viewers to revel in the colors, patterns, and shapes of individual pans rather than to be distracted by the chaos of an arbitrary display or the elaborate schema of a highly calculated hang.

Wurtz's resourcefulness—his tactic of making-do while making—emphasizes self-reliance and manual skills, two of the defining characteristics of DIY culture, which flowered in postwar America in spite of, or more likely because of, the industrial appetite for mass production. The artist notes that his own methodology for the *Pan Paintings* involves mining the very products that mechanization proliferated: "While I do make objects—in a way it would be more accurate to say that I rearrange objects that already exist."[9] Wurtz's "rearrangement" manifests in how he applies color to each pan in accordance with the preexisting parameters of its stamped

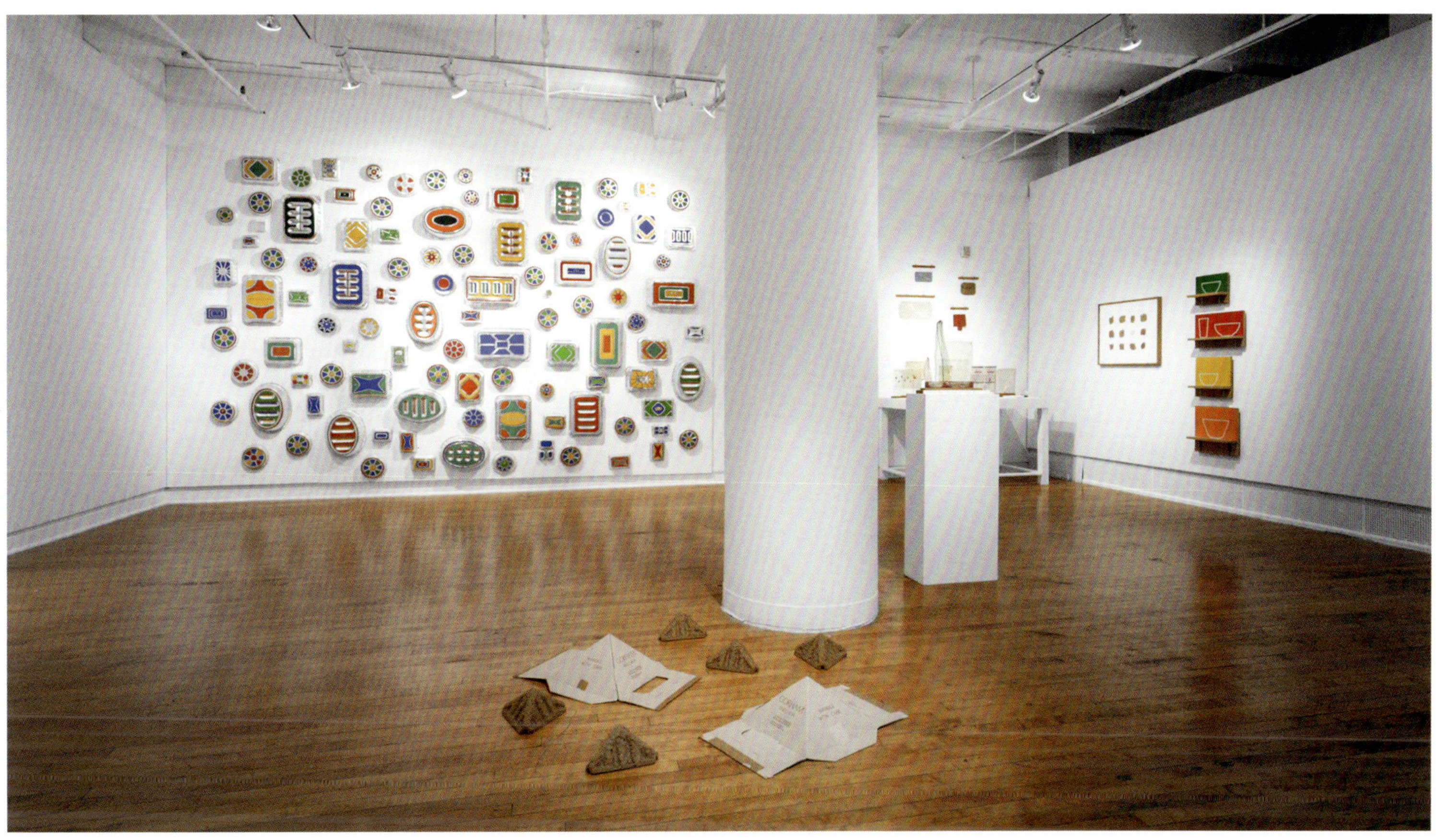

design. In one instance, the bottom of a circular pan is embossed with a sunburst arrangement that the artist embellished with blazing orange for the inner "sun" and outer "halo," along with fluorescent green for the seven "rays" (plate 56). Painting the pans thus is both duplicative (reiterating the industrial template of impressed shapes with planes of color), and distinctive (given the formal decision-making involved: which color[s]; what manner of application).

These works—neither merely reproducible nor wholly unique—carry on an American mode of production in the arts, a mode that art historian Katy Siegel claims (in relation to historical figures like Cahill and more contemporary artists such as Allen Ruppersberg and Richard Prince) blurs "the line between maker and consumer, professional and amateur, and even combine[s] the seeming antithesis of reproduction and DIY hand-making."[10]

Such blurring became especially prominent with the craft-oriented ethos of the 1950s, when average Americans—incentivized by the new reality of financial solvency and increased mechanization of daily chores—searched for ways to be more productive with their leisure hours. The consumer market responded to this mass phenomenon of newly impassioned hobbyists: paint-by-number sets, for example, which had previously been marketed only to children, became available for adults, with templates now drawn "by real artists," as one manufacturer proudly advertised.[11]

These kits were one among many forms of art instruction—including TV programming, mailed lessons, and specialized equipment—directed at the masses and targeted for individual consumption at home. And while some carefully followed paint-by-number guidelines to produce faithful copies and to master technical skills—hewing to that Deweyian belief, pervasive

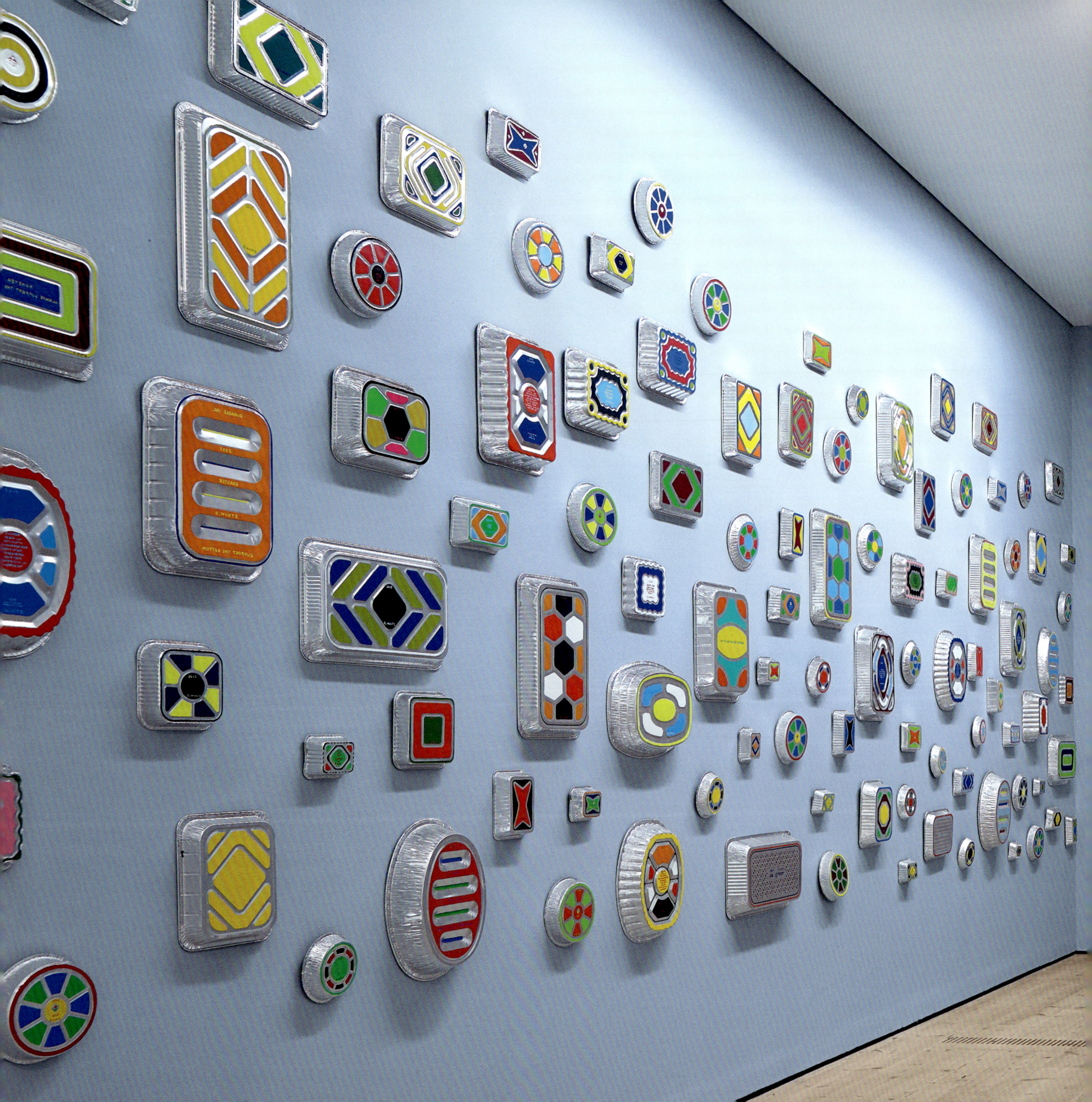

in America, of learning by doing—there was also artistic competency to be gained through deviation. "The real art began the moment the hobbyist ignored outlines to blend adjacent colors, added or dropped a detail, or elaborated upon a theme by extending the composition onto the frame," writes curator William L. Bird Jr. in a catalogue essay accompanying his Smithsonian exhibition *Paint by Number* in 2001; thus, "by doing what art was not supposed to be, one could learn what it was."[12] And then there were others, principally art educators, who decried such commercial forms of didactic art as a wholesale threat to individual imagination. "In extending the standardizing influence of the machine to his leisure time activities the easily deceived squelches his native urge for creative self-expression, and yields to the destructive powers that regiment and ruin the soul of man," wrote one such educator for the *School Arts Magazine*.[13]

■ ■ □

No artist seemed better primed to critique this contested terrain around numbered paint kits than Andy Warhol, who worked as a successful commercial illustrator before beginning to show his artwork in galleries in the late 1950s. From 1962 to 1963, the artist produced the *Do-It-Yourself* series, a group of five paintings—two still lifes, two seascapes, and one landscape—based on actual templates from paint-by-number sets. In *Do-It-Yourself (Landscape)* (1962), Warhol highlights the prescriptive nature of this programmed painting by leaving various outlined sections of roads, lawns, foliage, and rooftops without color—but with numbers visible, as if in conscious pursuit of a half-learned lesson. The work's ostensible status as "in progress" invites viewers to consider the ease of completing the painting by merely following the numbered system. And yet this subtle suggestion that "you can do it, too" is ultimately cheeky: Warhol hand-painted all aspects of each composition, including the lines and numbers of the faux template. Warhol thus re-created a paint-by-number diagram not only by refusing to "complete" the painting, but also by insisting on manual techniques for the instructional components, thereby quietly subtending the readymade aesthetic with the handmade.

Rather than indulging in nostalgic mimicry of these hobbyist kits—whose 1950s heyday had become a distant memory by the 1960s—

Warhol's *Do-It-Yourself* series embodies his cagey attitude toward capitalist culture in America, suggesting that independent thought and individual creativity can still exist within the bounds of commodified experience and prefabricated art, and perhaps even thrive there. Such an attitude bears the imprint of Marcel Duchamp's legacy, particularly his tactic in the late 1910s of selecting manufactured objects and titling, dating, and presenting them as a category of art ("readymades") within institutional contexts. At times, Duchamp slightly modified these utilitarian items—for example, mounting a bicycle wheel upside-down on a kitchen stool in 1913 for *Bicycle Wheel*—and referred to these works as "assisted readymades." Whereas Duchamp's production of readymades liberated the hand from manual craftsmanship—thus diminishing the traditional role of the artist as skilled creator—Warhol's *Do-It-Yourself* series presented a twist to such decision-making procedures: his virtuosic fabrication of the appearance of mass-produced templates crystallized the paradox of these paintings as "handmade readymades."

Wurtz's "rearrangement" of aluminum pans contains Duchampian overtones; his abstract works, borrowing preexisting compositions from the stamped bottoms of factory-made pans, are hand-painted depictions of industrial patterns. For *Untitled (pan painting)* (2014, see frontispiece), Wurtz chose a palette of five colors—black, white, and the three primaries—for a rectangular pan with a stamped pattern of hexagonal shapes akin to the organic structure of beehives. The resulting work treats each hexagon as a flat plane of pure color—a mode of abstraction reminiscent of the work of Piet Mondrian, whose paintings of the early twentieth century feature asymmetrical arrangements of geometric shapes in unmodulated primary colors. Wurtz's evocation of Mondrian is chiefly visual—a look of modernism familiar to the eyes, but divergent in conception. Whereas Mondrian envisioned his abstract paintings as registering a universal pictorial language (other early modernists espoused similar idealism in their lofty discussions of color symbolism and formal spirituality), Wurtz positions his *Pan Paintings* in a more workaday stratum, superimposing historical lineages of abstraction atop utilitarian objects.

His style of painting recalls "hard-edge abstraction"—a term initially applied to the work of painters in the 1960s, many based on the West Coast, who filled geometric figures with monochromatic fields of unmodulated color. In opposition to the gestural marks of the Abstract Expressionists, which were intended to convey the artist's subjectivity, such fields of flat color—smoothly brushed with clean edges—appear objective, effacing an artist's painterly touch. As with his oblique reference to Mondrian, Wurtz's emulation of hard-edge painting consciously teeters in certain respects. He does not use tape as a masking aid to achieve precise lines and sharp geometric shapes; instead, he embraces human error (e.g., paint spilling over the contours of embossed forms), signaling his favorable estimation of handmade details and his own painterly touch (plates 38 and 52).

The modernist intention behind hard-edge abstraction—to intensify the intrinsic flatness of the picture plane—is unachievable, and perhaps even undesirable, for Wurtz; his "canvas," i.e., the surface of the pan's bottom, is not flat, but rather bumpy and dimensional from imprinted patterns. And yet, these works do not reside in the fraught terrain between painting and sculpture; they do not fly the banner of painting-as-object for the sake of challenging discrete art-historical categories. Notably, Wurtz focuses his application of paint to the bottom surface—a single plane, even if embossed—instead of the pan in its entirety. (While the pans' external shapes matter in the series overall, the artist's principal concern is for the stamped patterns of the pans' bottoms.) The artist's approach to abstraction probes not what his *Pan Paintings* are and how they can be classified, but rather what they do and how they behave in the world of art in general.

■ ■ ■

Wurtz's abstractions are not *of* something, but rather inhere *in* the objects themselves. The punched-out shapes of boomerangs, squares, trapezoids, and circles, and the imprinted lines—straight, short, curved, long, or zigzagging—exist under the vague guise of utilitarian use: perhaps these textured surfaces offer an alternative to pans with nonstick coating; perhaps they provide a reservoir for liquid when braising; perhaps they add structure that strengthens the thin and lightweight metal; or perhaps they keep fried food crisp by collecting excess oil. With neither overriding consumer consensus nor explicit explanation outlined by the pans' manufacturers, the unknown function of these textured surfaces easily remaps onto visual pleasure. Whatever their native purpose, these oven-ready compositions liberate Wurtz from being individually responsible for the design of his abstractions; they already exist in the world as anonymous and versatile creations available for public use.

"Everyday life invents itself by *poaching* in countless ways on the property of others," writes scholar Michel de Certeau, aptly describing the relentless flow of appropriation in our daily existence.[14] Wurtz's recycling of disposable pans aligns with de Certeau's description of consumption as an intriguing mode of production that "insinuates itself everywhere, silently and almost invisibly, because it does not manifest itself through its own products, but rather through its *ways of using* the products imposed by a dominant economic order."[15] In effect, Wurtz's *Pan Paintings* render the artist as both consumer—poaching these pans' anonymously designed patterns— as well as a producer, by his "ways of using" these patterns as templates for abstract paintings. In closing the gap between makers and consumers of culture, this body of work exercises a model of reciprocity endemic to amateur culture in America; that is, reciprocity operating through earnest exchange and without an underlying intent to subvert or obscure the source. Or, rather, with overriding intent to strike a "balance," as Wurtz explained in a 2016 interview: "What I like about [the *Pan Paintings*] is that they are mass-produced, the designs are all made by someone anonymous, so it's really important that the painting is done by me. The balance has to be right."[16]

In salvaging these throwaway pans for works of art, Wurtz underscores the American tradition of making do with what we have by investing in quotidian items—of drawing out their life-affirming qualities. While his application of bold color vivifies the industrial templates—and, in turn, the anonymous designers behind them—there is equal vitality in the act of viewing these *Pan Paintings* in substantial groupings on the gallery wall or in the pages of this book. The variety of sizes and shapes in aluminum pans, from small circles to large ovals and perfect squares to subdivided rectangles, registers the breadth of contexts in which such containers might appear: single-serve TV dinner, backyard barbecue, Thanksgiving potluck, restaurant delivery, unfussy wedding buffet, leftover lunch at work, book-club spread, or church-basement support gathering. Whether providing food for one or many, in public or in private, these containers attest to daily nourishment; their capacity to also exist as ready-made abstractions reminds us that art partakes in such everyday sustenance, deepening our access to body and soul—and to each other.

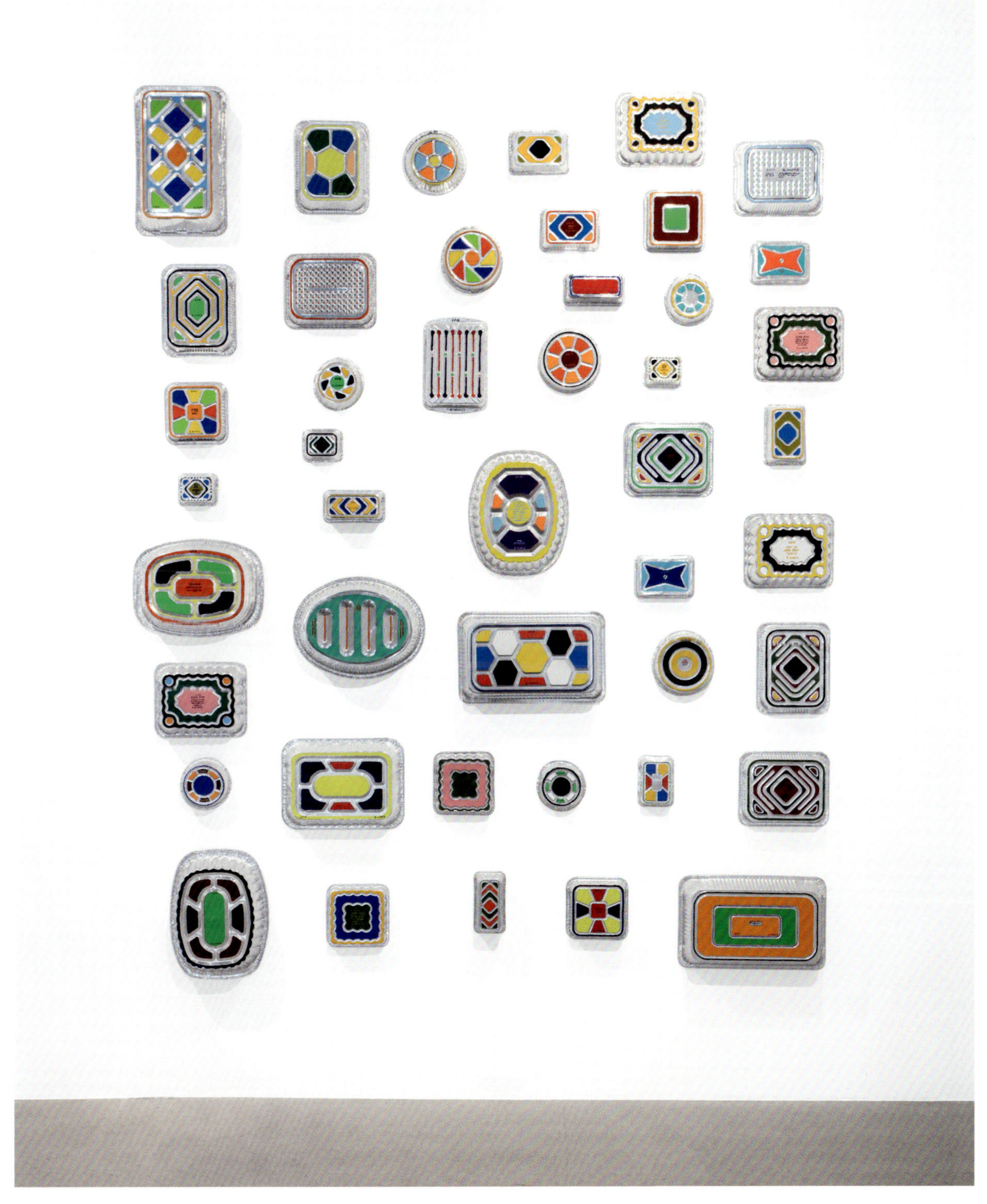

Fig 5

NOTES

1 B. Wurtz, "You've Got to Start Somewhere: B. Wurtz in Conversation with Laurence Sillars," in *B. Wurtz: Selected Works 1970–2015*, ed. Laurence Sillars, exh. cat. (Gateshead, UK: Baltic Centre for Contemporary Art, 2016), 96.

2 Wurtz, "You've Got to Start Somewhere," 96.

3 Wurtz claims that he identified these categories, more or less, in an early and seminal work, *Three Important Things* (1973), in which he scrawled the title on paper, listing underneath: "1. Sleeping / 2. Eating / 3. Keeping warm." Bruce Hainley, "Only Connect: The Art of B. Wurtz" in *B. Wurtz: Selected Works 1970–2015*, 12.

4 Scholar and curator Lynne Cooke provides a masterful account of Holger Cahill and the Index of American Design in "Boundary Trouble: Navigating Margin and Mainstream" in *Outliers and American Vanguard Art*, ed. Lynne Cooke, exh. cat. (Washington, DC: National Gallery of Art; Chicago: University of Chicago Press, 2018), 7–8. She also explores the difficulties in grasping terms that denote artistic training; e.g., "self-taught" devolved from favorable to denigrating since many who lacked formal academic training still felt that they had earned "credentials" by "maturing in cosmopolitan art circles" and were therefore not autodidacts. Cooke, "Boundary Trouble," 25n4.

5 *OED Online*, s.v. amateur, Oxford University Press, March 2020, www.oed.com/view/Entry/6041.

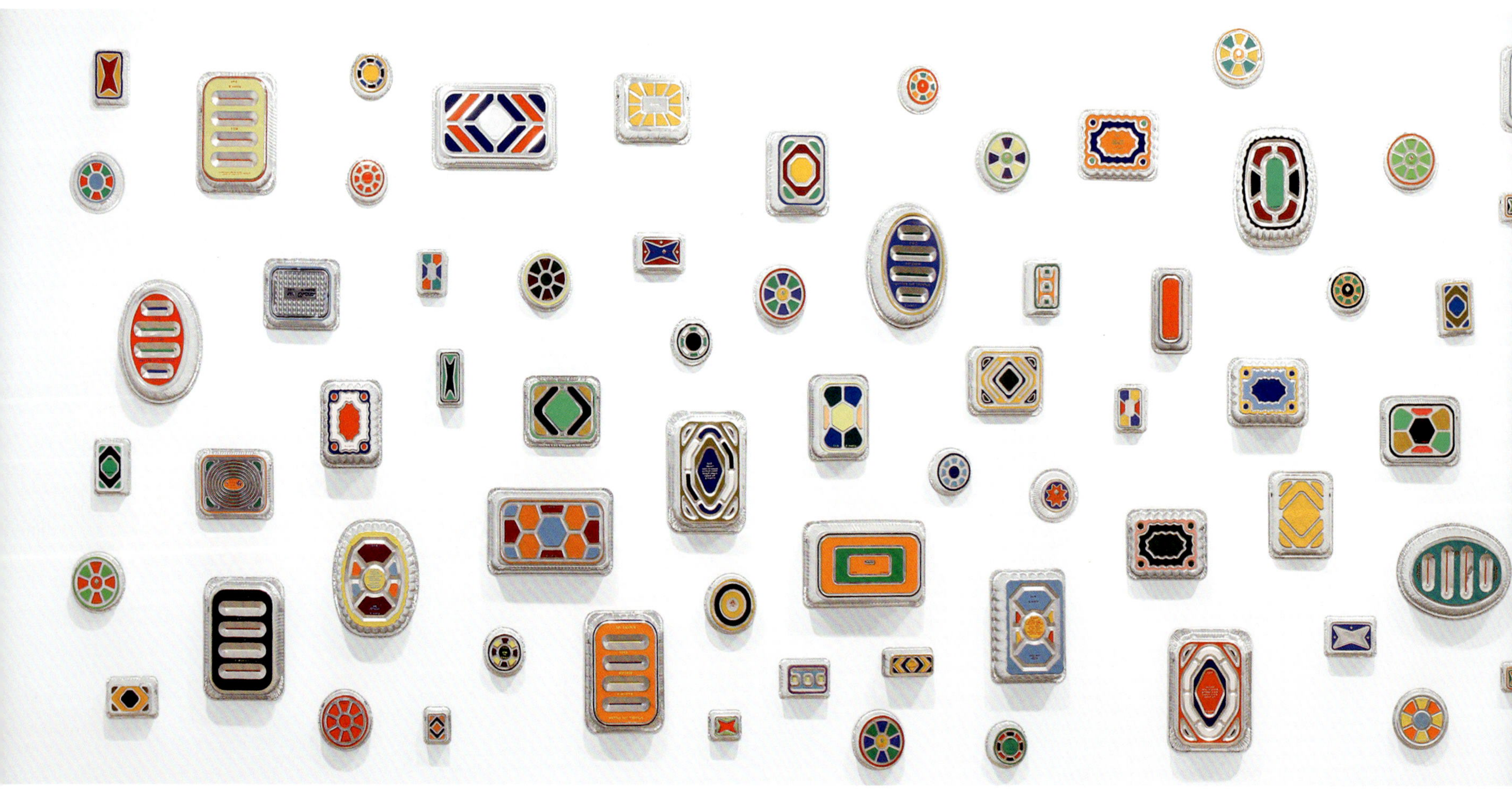

6 Howard Singerman, *Art Subjects: Making Artists in the American University* (Berkeley, CA: University of California Press, 2010), 129–30.

7 Allan Kaprow, "The Artist as a Man of the World" (1964) in *Essays on the Blurring of Art and Life*, ed. Jeff Kelley (Berkeley, CA: University of California Press, 2003), 51.

8 Kaprow, "The Artist as a Man of the World," 58.

9 Wurtz cited in Hainley, "Only Connect: The Art of B. Wurtz," 12.

10 Katy Siegel, *Since '45: America and the Making of Contemporary Art* (London: Reaktion Books, 2011), 172.

11 The manufacturer Picture Craft quoted in Karal Ann Marling, *As Seen on TV: The Visual Culture of Everyday Life in the 1950s* (Cambridge, MA: Harvard University Press, 1994), 65.

12 William L. Bird Jr., ed., *Paint By Number*, exh. cat. (New York: Princeton Architectural Press, 2001), 17.

13 Kenneth D. Winebrenner, "Creative Citizens," *School Arts Magazine*, no. 54 (May 1955): 48.

14 Michel de Certeau, *The Practice of Everyday Life*, trans. Steven F. Rendall (Berkeley, CA: University of California Press, 1984), xii.

15 De Certeau, *The Practice of Everyday Life*, xiii.

16 "B. Wurtz with Sara Roffino," *Brooklyn Rail*, June 4, 2016, accessed May 7, 2020, https://brooklynrail.org/2016/06/art/b-wurtz-with-sara-roffino.

I DEDICATE THIS ESSAY TO MY DAUGHTER, ISADORA LOU KULOK, WHO WAS CONCEIVED AND BORN ALL ALONGSIDE THE DEVELOPMENT OF THIS BOOK; MY EVERYDAY IS MORE REMARKABLE BECAUSE OF YOU.

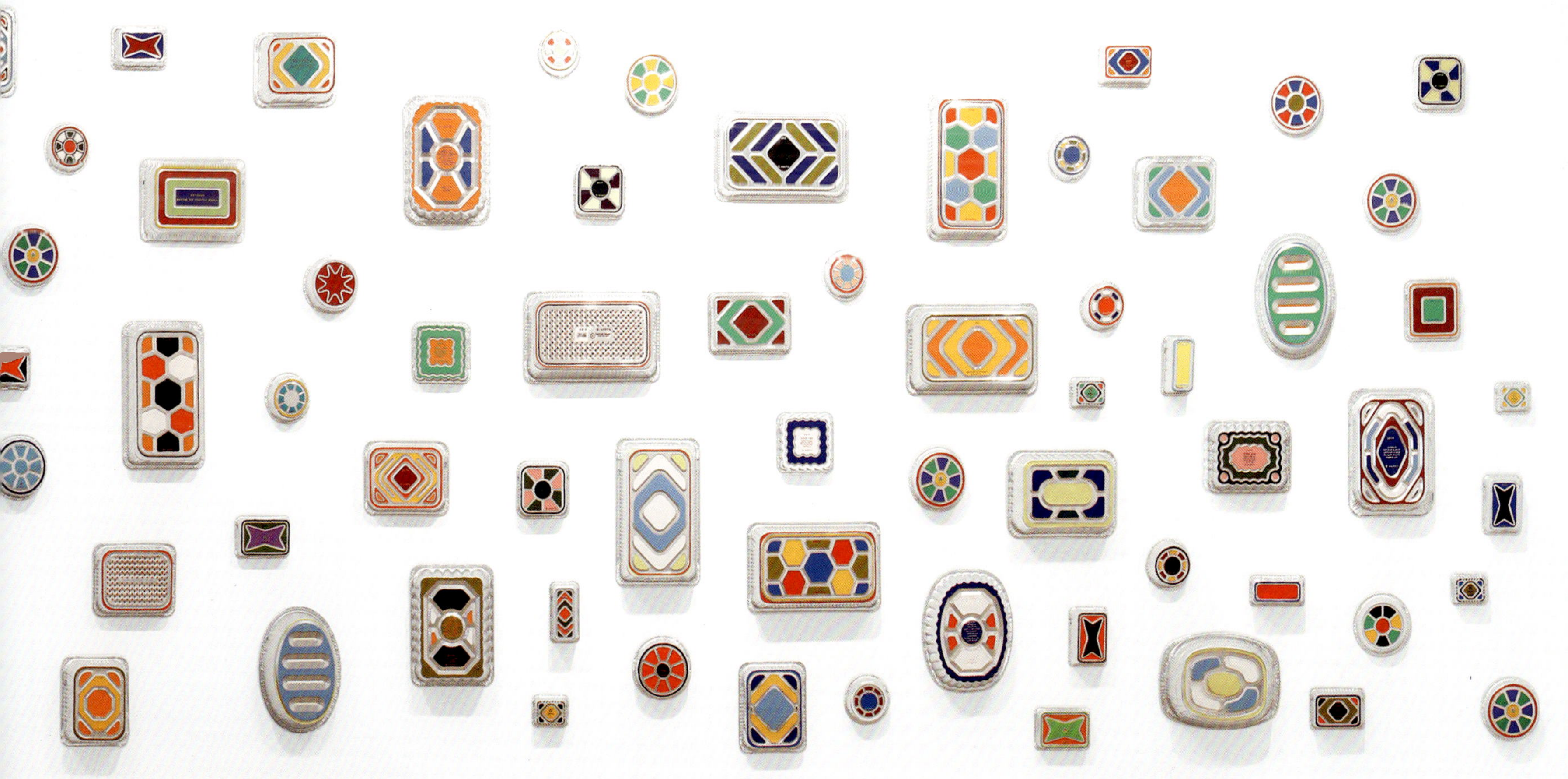

PLATES

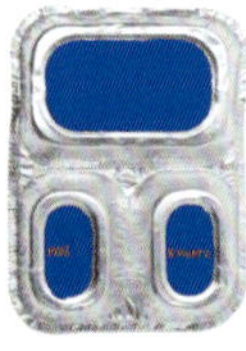

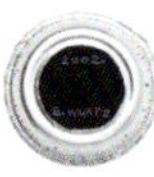

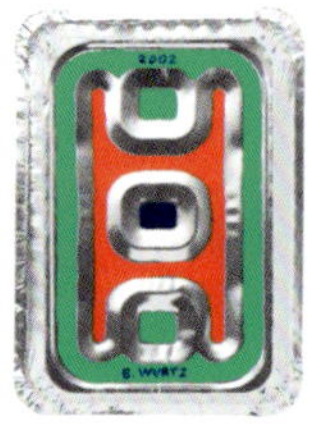

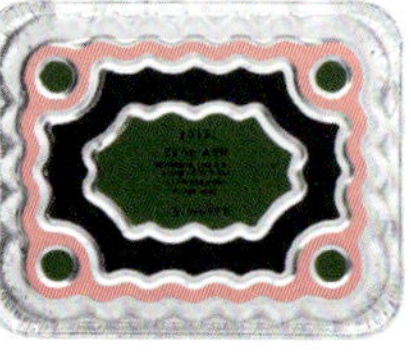

1 8.5 x 6.25 x 1.5″ (1996)   **2** 3.25 x 3.25 x 1.5″ (2002)   **3** 8.5 x 6 x 2″ (2002)   **4** 10.5 x 12.75 x 2.5″ (2015)

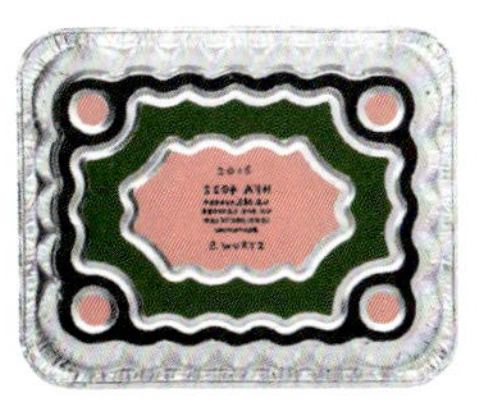

5 10.5 x 12.75 x 2.5" (2015)

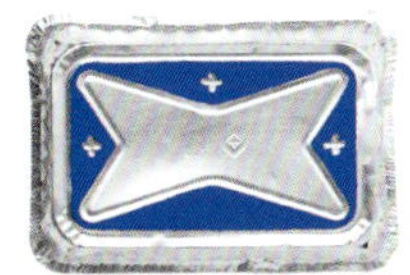

6 6 x 8.5 x 2" (1992)

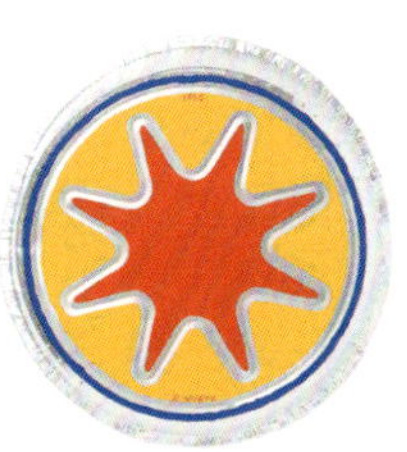

7 8.5 x 8.5 x 1.75" (1992)

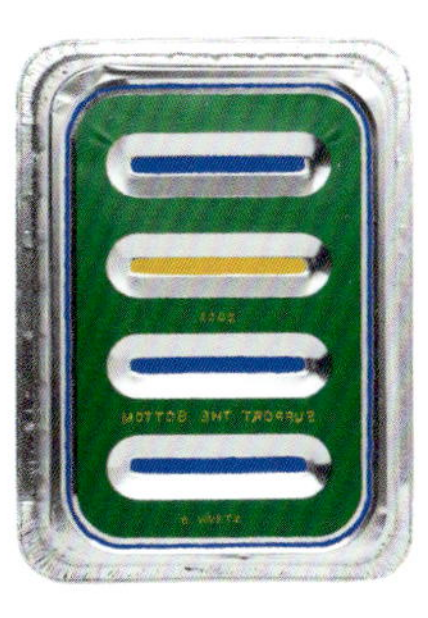

8 12.5 x 20.75 x 3" (2014)

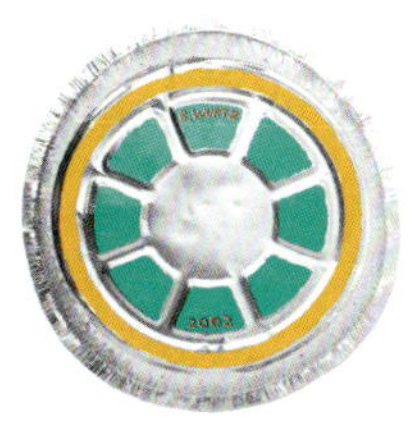

9 7.25 x 7.25 x 1.75" (2002)

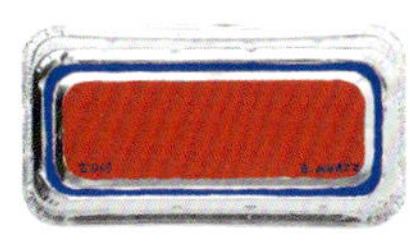

10 4.5 x 8.75 x 2.5" (2015)

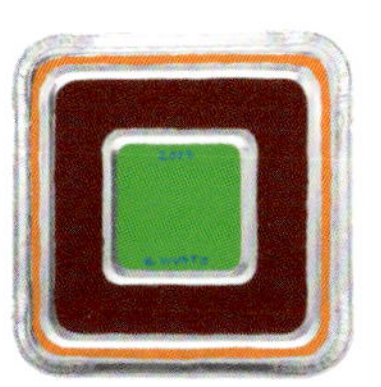

11 8.75 x 8.75 x 1.5" (2014)

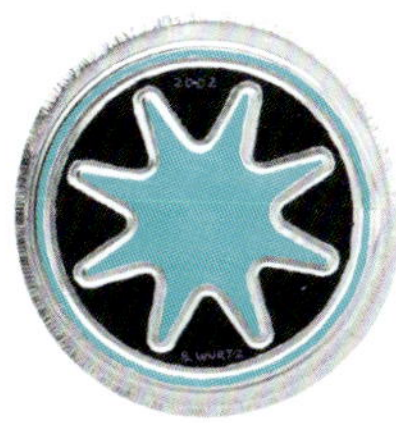

12 8.5 x 8.5 x 1.75" (2002)

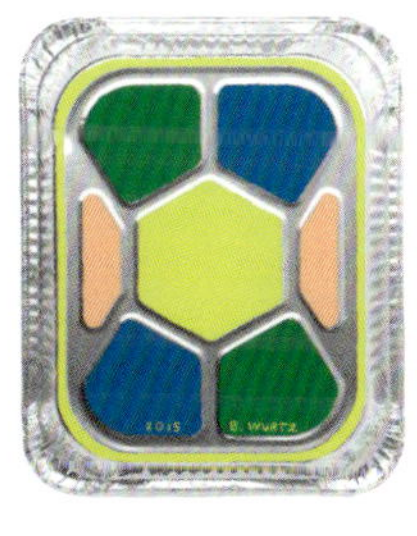

13 12.75 x 10.25 x 2.5" (2015)

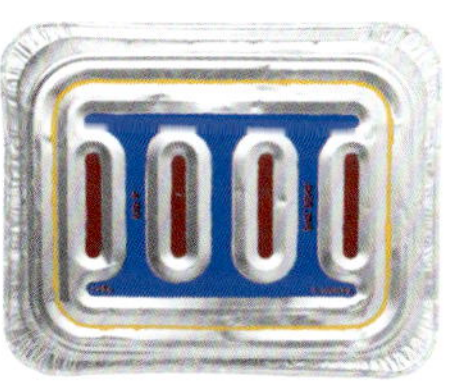

14 10.25 x 12.75 x 1.75" (1996)

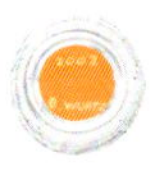

15 3.25 x 3.25 x 1.5" (2002)

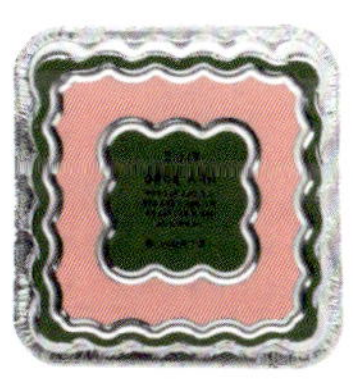

16 8.75 x 8.75 x 1.5" (2015)

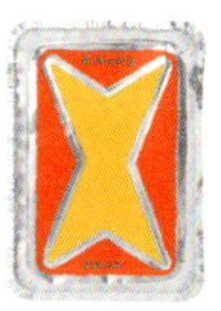

17 8.5 x 6 x 2" (2002)

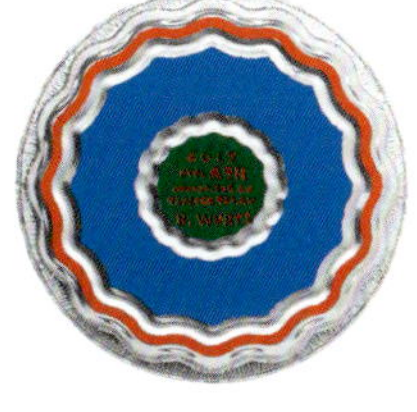

18 9 x 9 x 1.5" (2019)

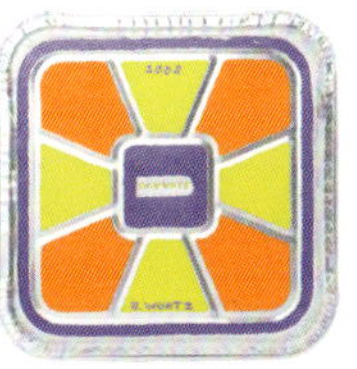

19 8.75 x 8.75 x .2" (2002)

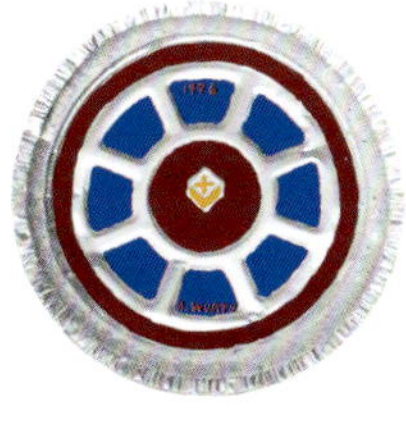

20 7.25 x 7.25 x 2.5" (1996)

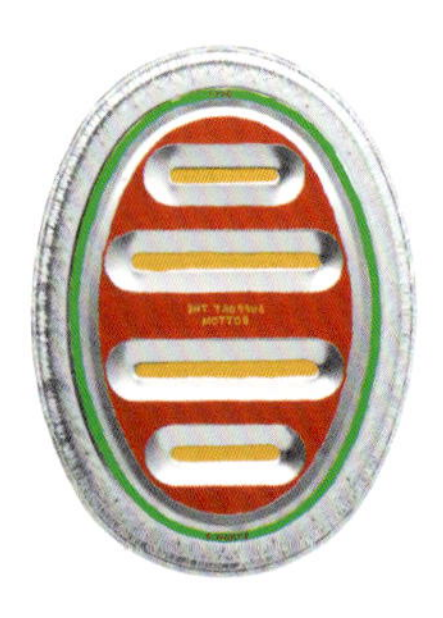

21 18.5 x 14 x 4" (1996)

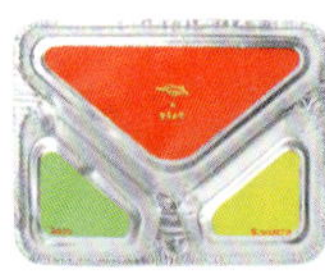

22 7 x 9 x 1.25" (2002)

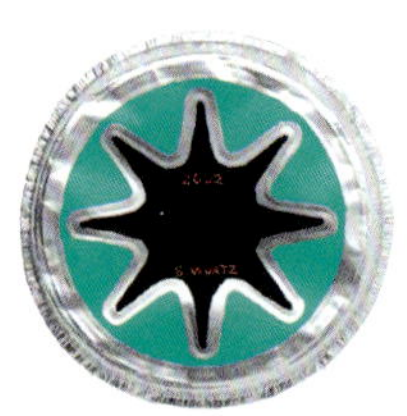

23 8.5 x 8.5 x 1.75" (2002)

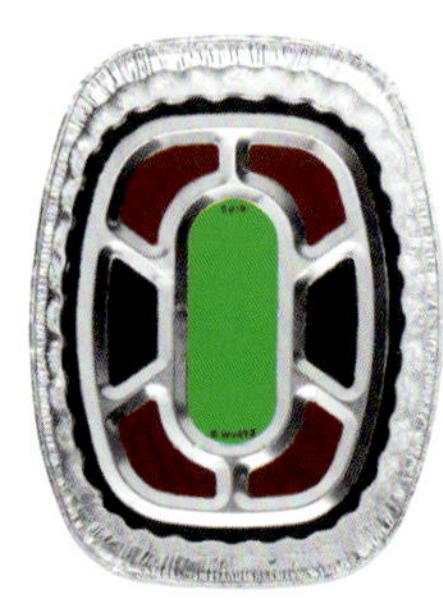

24 18.5 x 13.75 x 3.25" (2014)

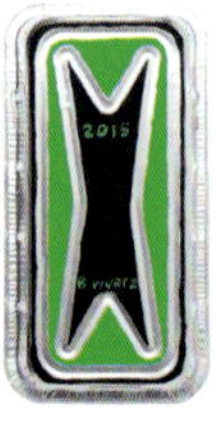

25 8.75 x 4.5 x 2.5" (2015)

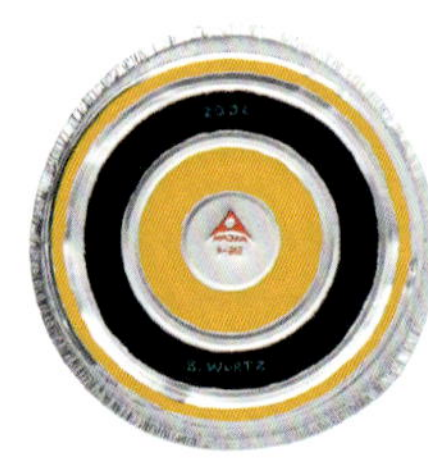

26 9 x 9 x 1.75" (2002)

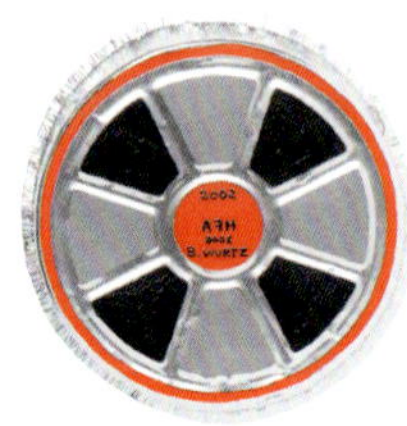

27 9 x 9 x 1.75" (2002)

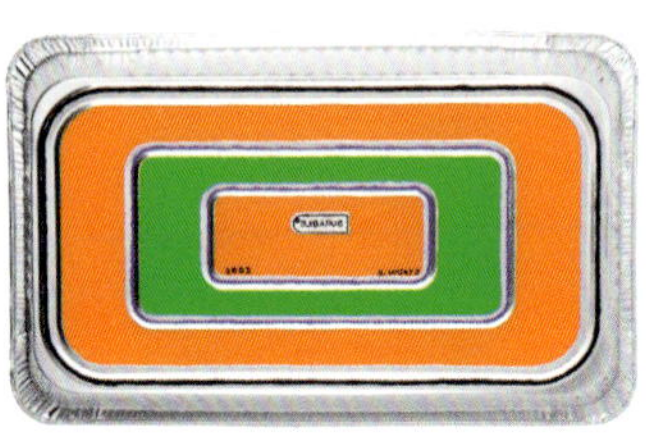

28 13 x 20.75 x 1.75 (2002)

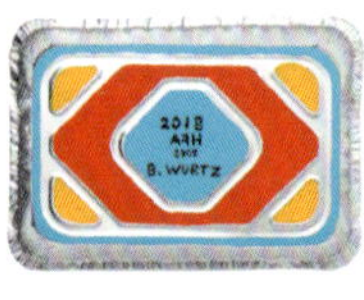

29 6 x 8.5 x 2" (2018)

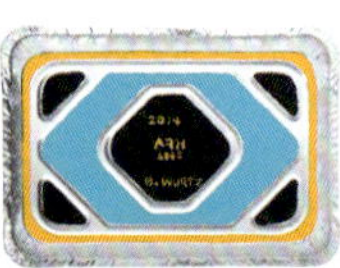

30 6 x 8.5 x 2" (2014)

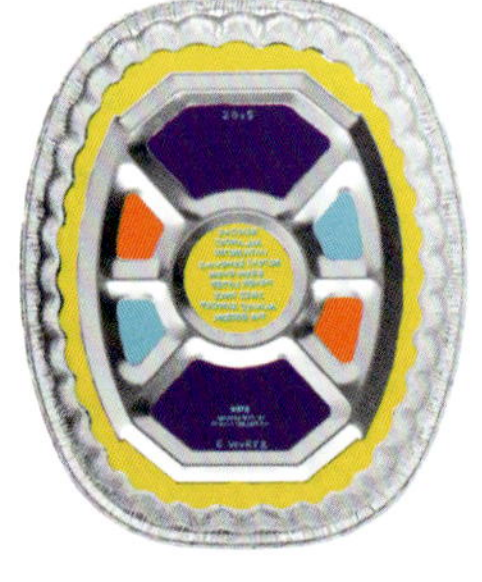

31 17.5 x 14.25 x 3" (2015)

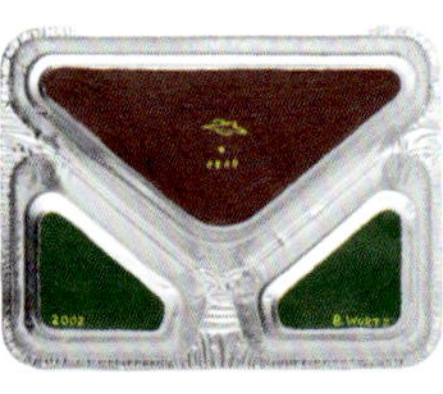

32 7 x 9 x 1.25" (2002)

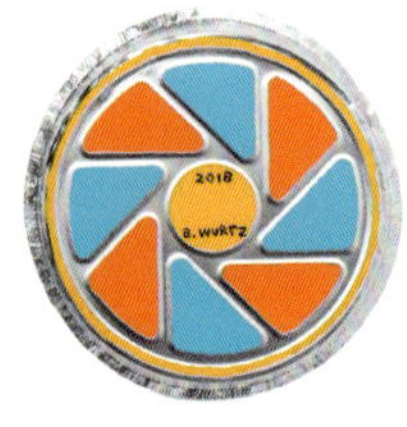

33 7.25 x 7.25 x 2.5" (2018)

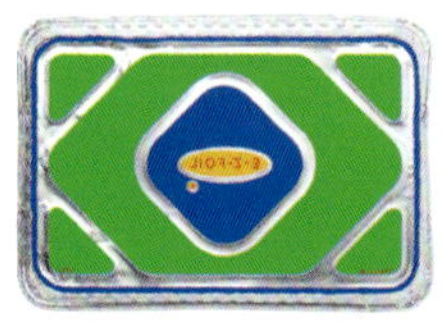

34 6 x 8.5 x 2" (1992)

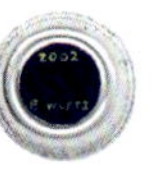

35 3.25 x 3.25 x 1.5" (2002)

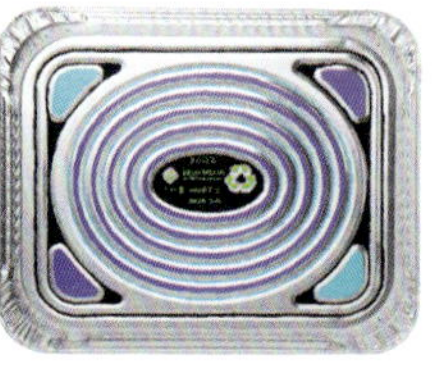

36 10.5 x 12.75 x 1.75" (2002)

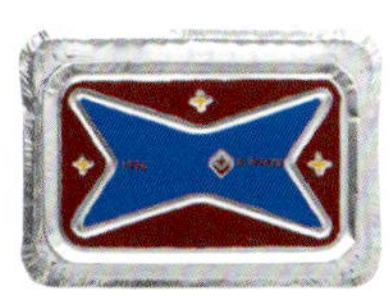

37 6 x 8.5 x 2" (1996)

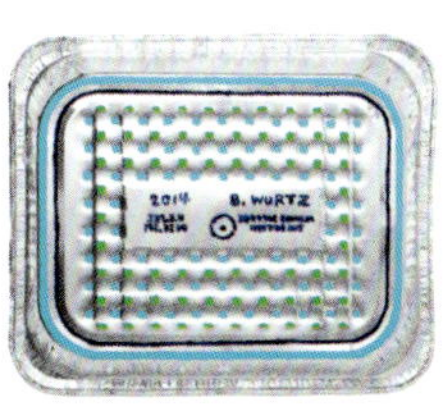

38 10.5 x 12.5 x 2.5" (2014)

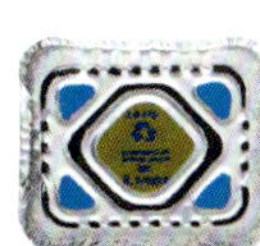

39 1.75 x 2.125 x .75" (2013)

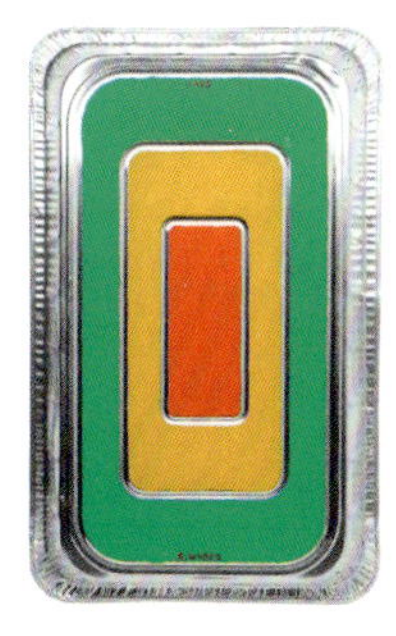

40 20.75 x 13 x 3.5" (1996)

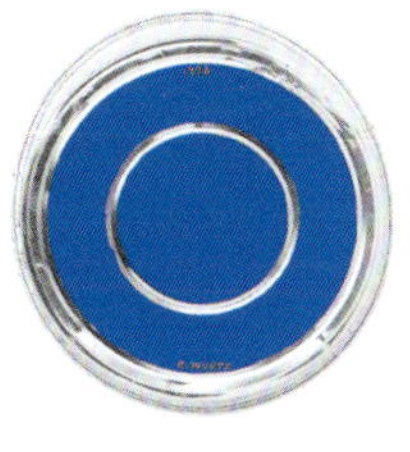

41 9 x 9 x 1.5" (1996)

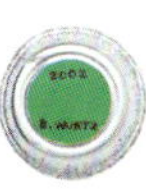

42 3.25 x 3.25 x 1.25" (2002)

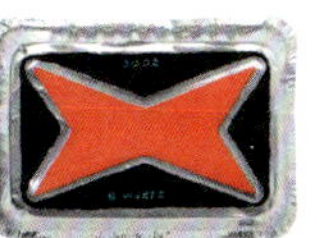

43 6 x 8.5 x 2" (2002)

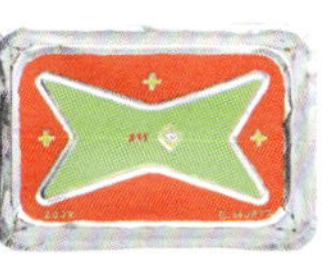

44 6 x 8.5 x 2" (2002)

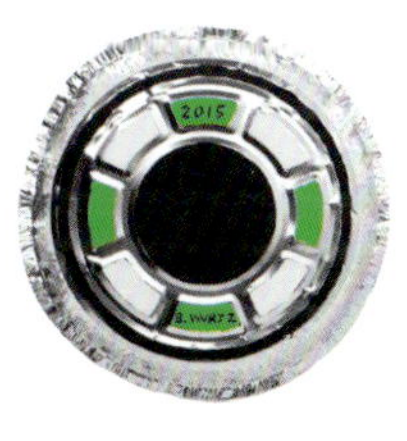

45 7 x 7 x 1.5" (2015)

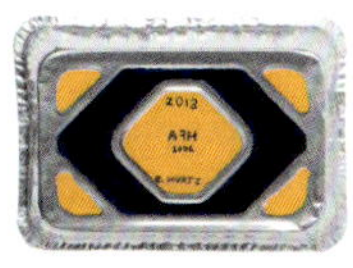

46 6 x 8.5 x 2" (2013)

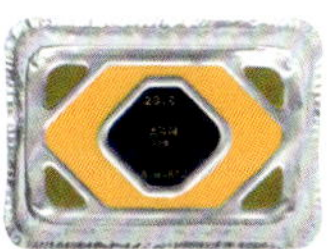

47 6 x 8.5 x 2" (2013)

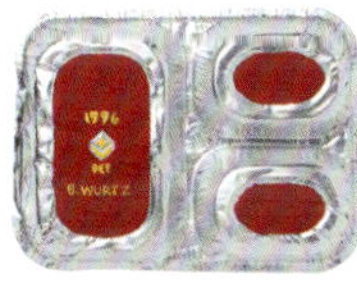

48 6.5 x 8.5 x 1.75" (1996)

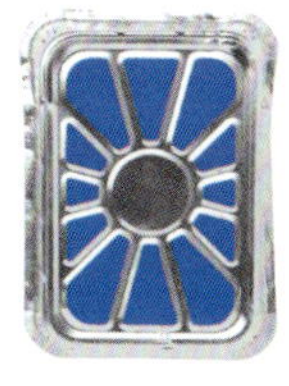

49 9.75 x 7 x 7.25" (1992)

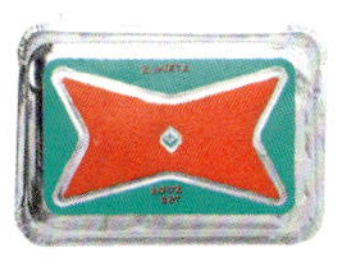

50 6 x 8.5 x 1.5" (2002)

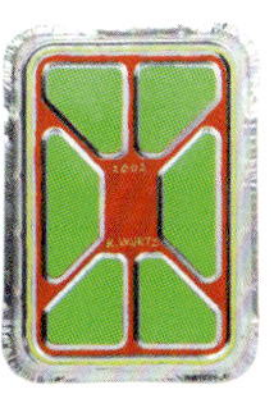

51 9.5 x 7 x 2.5" (2002)

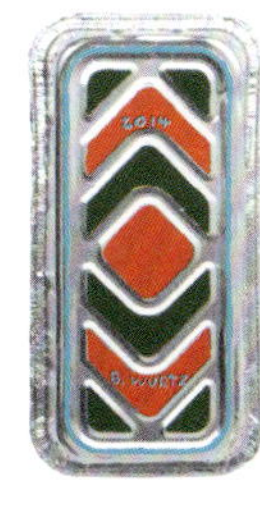

52 8.75 x 4.5 x 2.5 (2014)

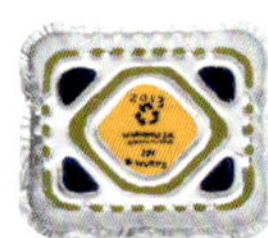

53 1.75 x 2.125 x .75" (2013)

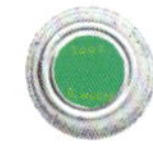

54 3.25 x 3.25 x 1.5" (2002)

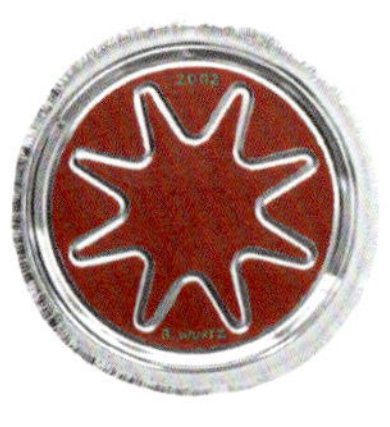

55 8.25 x 8.25 x 1.75" (2002)

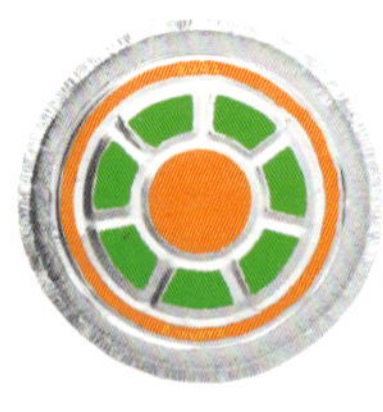

56 7.25 x 7.25 x 1.75 (2002)

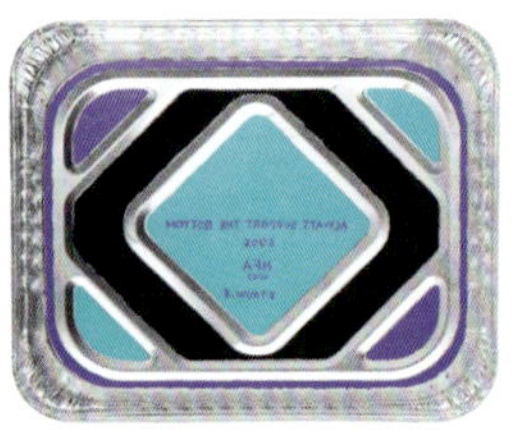

57 10.5 x 12.75 x 2.25" (2002)

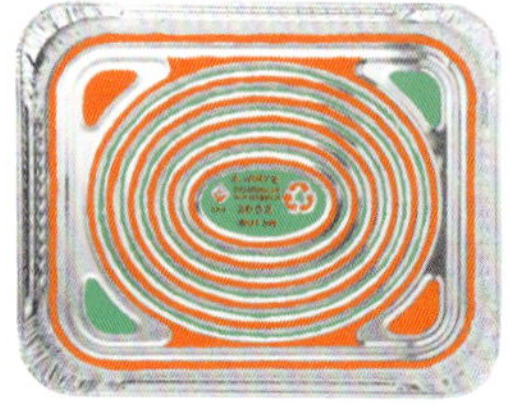

58 10.25 x 12.75 x 1.75" (2002)

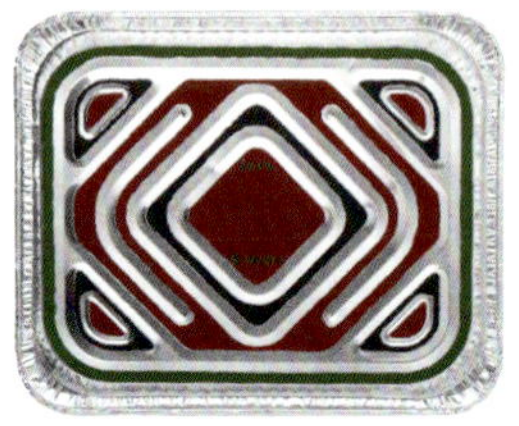

59 10.5 x 12.75 x 1.75" (2014)

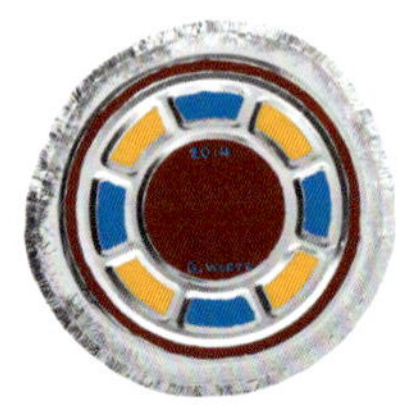

60 7.25 x 7.25 x 1.5" (2014)

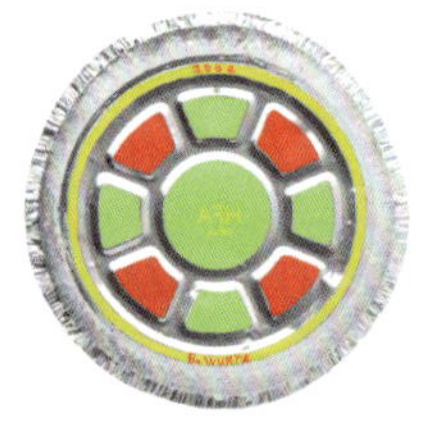

61 7.25 x 7.25 x 1.5" (2002)

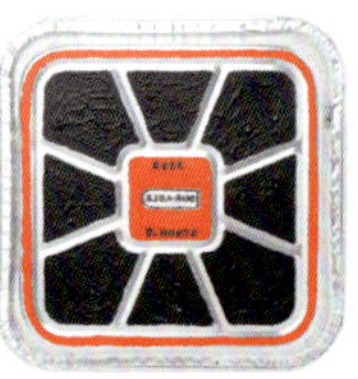

62 8.75 x 8.75 x 1.75" (2002)

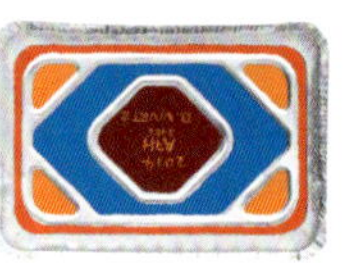

63 6 x 8.5 x 2" (2014)

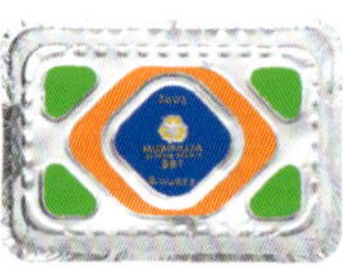

64 6 x 8.5 x 2" (2002)

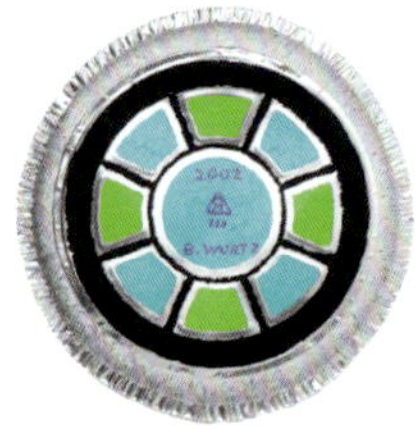

65 7.25 x 7.25 x 1.5 (2002)

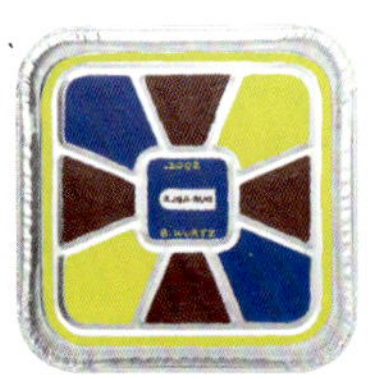

66 8.75 x 8.75 x 2" (2002)

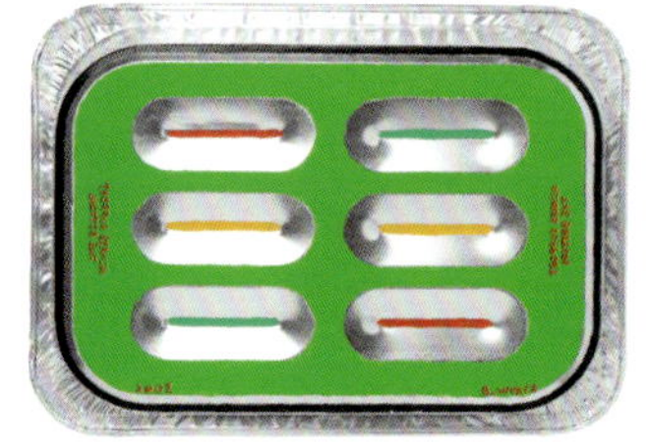

67 10.25 x 12.75 x 1.75" (2002)

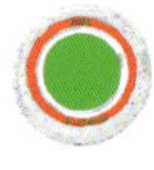

68 3.25 x 3.25 x 1.5" (1992)

FIGURES

1 INSTALLATION VIEW, *B. WURTZ*, KATE MACGARRY, LONDON, MAY 30–JULY 12, 2019; PHOTOGRAPH BY ANGUS MILL © 2019 KATE MACGARRY.

2 INSTALLATION VIEW, *B. WURTZ: FOUR COLLECTIONS,* THE ALDRICH CONTEMPORARY ART MUSEUM, RIDGEFIELD, CT MAY 3–OCTOBER 25, 2015; PHOTOGRAPH BY CHAD KLEITSCH © 2015 THE ALDRICH CONTEMPORARY ART MUSEUM.

3 INSTALLATION VIEW, *B. WURTZ: 70 + 30 = 2000,* GALLERY 400, UNIVERSITY OF ILLINOIS, CHICAGO, OCTOBER 2– OCTOBER 28, 2000; PHOTOGRAPH BY TOM VAN EYNDE © GALLERY 400.

4 INSTALLATION VIEW, *B. WURTZ: SELECTED WORKS, 1970–2015,* BALTIC CENTRE FOR CONTEMPORARY ART, GATESHEAD, UK, NOVEMBER 20, 2015–FEBRUARY 28, 2016; PHOTOGRAPH BY JOHN MCKENZIE © 2015 BALTIC.

5 INSTALLATION VIEW, *B. WURTZ: THIS HAS NO NAME,* INSTITUTE OF CONTEMPORARY ART, LOS ANGELES, SEPTEMBER 30, 2019–FEBRUARY 17, 2019; PHOTOGRAPH BY ELON SCHOENHOLZ © 2018 ICA LA.

6 INSTALLATION VIEW, *B. WURTZ: FOUR COLLECTIONS,* THE ALDRICH CONTEMPORARY ART MUSEUM, RIDGEFIELD, CT, MAY 3–OCTOBER 25, 2015; PHOTOGRAPH BY CHAD KLEITSCH © 2015 THE ALDRICH CONTEMPORARY ART MUSEUM.

*I would like to thank everyone
who helped get this book published.
Everyone!*
—B. Wurtz

Editor: Barney Kulok
Designer: Ann Bobco
Text Editor: Claire Lehmann
Post Production: Eli Durst
Prepress: ARTPRODUCT

All Artworks © B. Wurtz
"Oven-Ready-Made" © Erica Cooke

Covers, frontispiece, and plates photographed by Barney Kulok.

Compilation, including selection, placement, and order of text
and images © 2020 Hunters Point Press. All rights reserved under
International and Pan-American Copyright Conventions. No part of this
publication may be reproduced or transmitted in any form whatsoever
without prior permission in writing from the publisher.

A very special thanks to Jill & Peter Kraus and Steel Stillman & Jane
Ayers for their generous support of this project.

First Edition, 2020

ISBN: 978-0-578-57691-6
Library of Congress Control Number: 2020934284

Printed in Spain by SYL L'art Gràfic
Distributed by Artbook/D.A.P.

Hunters Point Press
4711 Vernon Boulevard
Long Island City, NY 11101
www.hunterspointpress.com